T0170431

Days and Memory

Charlotte Delbo

Days and Memory

Translated from the French
and with a preface by Rosette Lamont

TMP

The Marlboro Press/Northwestern
Northwestern University Press
Evanston, Illinois

The Marlboro Press/Northwestern
Northwestern University Press
Evanston, Illinois 60208-4210

Originally published in French under the title
La mémoire et les jours by Berg international
éditeurs, Paris. Copyright © 1985 by Berg
international éditeurs, Paris. English translation
copyright © 1990 by Rosette Lamont.
First published 1990 by the Marlboro Press.
This edition published 2001 by the Marlboro
Press/Northwestern. All rights reserved.

Printed in the United States of America

10 9 8 7 6 5 4 3 2 1

ISBN 0-8101-6090-0

Library of Congress Cataloging-in-Publication Data

Delbo, Charlotte.
    [Mémoire et les jours. English]
    Days and memory / Charlotte Delbo ; translated
and with a preface by Rosette Lamont.
    p. cm.
    ISBN 0-8101-6090-0 (pbk. : alk. paper)
    1. Auschwitz (Concentration camp)—Literary
collections. 2. World War, 1939–1945—
Literary collections. I. Title.
PQ2664.E5117 M413 2001
848'.91409—dc21
                                    2001042567

The paper used in this publication meets the
minimum requirements of the American
National Standard for Information Sciences—
Permanence of Paper for Printed Library
Materials, ANSI Z39.48-1984.

Contents

When I first met Charlotte Delbo some twenty years ago, I was struck by a quality of presence I had never encountered before. Tall, so erect as to seem almost stiff-backed, with the straight nose and proud neck of a remorseless Electra and a Parisian *faubourg* accent that I associated with the actress Arletty, the woman facing me was a study in contrasts: part heroic Greek princess, part Gavroche. It was she, however, who was taking me in. Her greenish-grey eyes, intense yet reserved, were plunging into mine, as if searching for some elusive answer. Strangely enough, I did not feel uncomfortable under this gaze, yet I knew I was either going to pass muster or be swept aside without appeal.

I had been brought to 33, rue Lacépède—Charlotte's modern two-room apartment above the tiled roofs and chimneys of this ancient Paris neighborhood—by Cynthia Haft, a graduate student of mine then working on her doctoral thesis on "The Theme of Nazi Concentration Camps in French Literature." The subject had emerged from Cynthia's years of acquaintance with Delbo, a valiant woman and Auschwitz survivor. As an adolescent girl, Cynthia had met Charlotte at a family-type American summer camp where the French visitor was giving some language courses. For the young girl this meeting was to have a determining effect upon the rest of her life.

That first day we started talking at once about Charlotte's own work and *la littérature concentrationnaire*. Charlotte explained what she had tried to do: *"Il faut donner à voir."* To show it for what it was; it was not an unambitious aim: to raise the image of the camps for all to see, in this generation and in all generations to come. The writers who have emerged from the concentration camp experience are natural classicists and moralists: they tend not to seek individual expression; but speak as interpreters for the survivors and on behalf of the dead.

For Delbo, writing, or even the prospect of writing some day, were she to survive, became her lifeline. She who had always loved books discovered in a new way the power of literature, harnessing it in order to use it, both for herself and for her companions, as a prime strategy for survival. Nor of course was she alone in this endeavor. The poet and scholar Frieda Aaron, a survivor of the Warsaw Ghetto uprising and of Maidanek, writes in her article "Yiddish and Polish Poetry in the Ghettos and Camps": "It was the process that helped to keep the soul alive." It was among the aims of the Nazi camps to bestialize human beings, to reduce them to filthy, diseased animals, lice-infested, stinking, dripping with dysentery, harrowed by unappeasable thirst. Under unimaginable conditions and threatened every instant by death it was almost impossible to keep hold of the realization that one had once enjoyed the privilege of being human, and of participating in some fashion, either as a listener, a reader or an active creator, in the *process* of transcending instinct through the higher emotions.

In her essay "Women Writers and the Holocaust," the critic Ellen S. Fine explains that "literature . . . became a means of mobilizing support systems and was part of a joint effort to stay alive." Recitation of poetry and singing occurred in such unlikely places as the camp infirmaries. Those who were able to return to their barracks continued this practice, prodding their memory to recapture whole poems and, in Charlotte's case, entire plays. Having formerly worked with the great French director Louis Jouvet, Delbo had kept a vivid, living memory of the plays she had watched him direct. Her barracks companions, however, being often from modest working class backgrounds, had in most cases never seen a play. In the evening, after an endless day of absurd toil in the frozen marshes, they would sit up on their tiered bunks, waiting like children for Charlotte's suggestion: "And now, let's go to the theater!" She would then proceed to recreate for her listeners one of the many plays she had watched come alive at the Athénée, Jouvet's theater. She would narrate some of the plot and act all the parts. Despite their exhaustion and the prospect of roll call before daybreak, the young women paid unfaltering attention, vowing, as Charlotte Delbo herself related to me, that, were they ever to return home to a normal life, they would make the effort to discover this splendid world of literature and drama which, during a brief moment's respite, enfolded them in its crimson-and-gold dream-image.

Hope may not cure malnutrition or preserve one from the bitter cold that turns blood to ice, but it helps a not yet inwardly destroyed person to retain some trace of human dignity. Memory is the faculty that enables this miracle to occur. It provides an essential fuel to the urge to go on living, to survive, to pass on the word. It operates in two ways: there is the remembering of the life one has left behind, and that remembrance strengthens; and their is a desire to build a memory bank upon which to draw in order to transmit to future generations an account of what one has endured. Thus, memory has both a personal and a collective dimension.

This I think is why Delbo used the word *memory* in the title of what was to be her final book, published shortly after her death as *La mémoire et les jours*. Even as she lay dying of lung cancer, Charlotte Delbo made of herself the living voice of memory, putting together the poems and sketches that contain, in concentrated form, a comprehensive picture of man's inhumanity to man (and to woman) in our time.

Days and Memory constitutes a series of vignettes, some written in the form of a monologue addressed to the invisible, attentive author, some in the form of a dialogue between the author and a friend. Some of the scenes and situations do indeed come from the German concentration camp experience, dominant throughout Delbo's previous writings; other moments and aspects of the Second World War appear in the sketches of the French police's round up of Paris Jews; of the uprising of the Warsaw ghetto and, also in Warsaw, of the Polish partisans; of the mass execution by the Germans of all the men in a Greek village. But also remembered are the events in Greece—and in Spain—that belong to the decades that followed the war. And

Days and Memory also includes the days, still closer to us, of the women of Buenos Aires who would assemble in the Plaza de Mayo to remember and protest the disappearance of their fathers, husbands and sons. Finally, the book ends with an appeal on behalf of the prisoners in the Soviet gulags, those most forgotten of the forgotten.

Charlotte Delbo's literary texts combine the honesty and objectivity of testimony with the particular conciseness of an art created on the edge of silence. In form and spirit it is not unrelated to Beckett's minimalist "dramaticules." When I told her in the course of that first visit that I considered her writings to be metaphysical, she looked at me with surprise. I tried to explain that her texts, issuing from a reality so extreme, seemed to me to reach beyond the bounds of what we know as ordinary life on our planet. They were located, I felt, in outer reaches, in a universe *in extremis*.

None of Us Will Return was her first book, written immediately after her own liberation. She wrote it and then put it in a drawer. There it remained for twenty years before she took it out and showed it to a publisher. It was as though, having enclosed her message in a bottle, she had not tossed it into the ocean but kept it with her, on her desert island. She told me: "I wanted to make sure it would withstand the test of time, since it had to travel far into the future."

Before she died she knew that one of her close friends and admirers was going to see to the publication of her final book. *Days and Memory* is Charlotte Delbo's ultimate message.

ROSETTE LAMONT

Days and Memory

Explaining the inexplicable. There comes to mind the image of a snake shedding its old skin, emerging from beneath it in a fresh, glistening one. In Auschwitz I took leave of my skin—it had a bad smell, that skin—worn from all the blows it had received, and found myself in another, beautiful and clean, although with me the molting was not as rapid as the snake's. Along with the old skin went the visible traces of Auschwitz: the leaden stare out of sunken eyes, the tottering gait, the frightened gestures. With the new skin returned the gestures belonging to an earlier life: the using of a toothbrush, of toilet paper, of a handkerchief, of a knife and fork, eating food calmly, saying hello to people upon entering a room, closing the door, standing up straight, speaking, later on smiling with my lips and, still later, smiling both at once with my lips and my eyes. Rediscovering odors, flavors, the smell of rain. In Birkenau, rain heightened the odor of diarrhea. It is the most fetid odor I know. In Birkenau, the rain came down upon the camp, upon us, laden with soot from the crematoriums, and with the odor of burning flesh. We were steeped in it.

It took a few years for the new skin to fully form, to consolidate.

Rid of its old skin, it's still the same snake. I'm the same too, apparently. However . . .

How does one rid oneself of something buried far within: memory and the skin of memory. It clings to me yet. Memory's skin has hardened, it allows nothing to filter out of what it retains, and I have no control over it. I don't feel it anymore.

In the camp one could never pretend, never take refuge in the imagination. I remember Yvonne Picart, a morning when we were carrying bricks from a wrecker's depot. We carried two bricks at a time, from one pile to another pile. We were walking side by side, our bricks hugged to our chests, bricks we had pried from a pile covered with ice, scraping our hands. Those bricks were heavy, and got heavier as the day wore on. Our hands were blue from cold, our lips cracked. Yvonne said to me: "Why can't I imagine I'm on the Boulevard Saint-Michel, walking to class with an armful of books?" and she propped the two bricks inside her forearm, holding them as students do books. "It's impossible. One can't imagine either being somebody else or being somewhere else."

I too, I often tried to imagine I was somewhere else. I tried to visualize myself as someone else, as when in a theatrical role you become another person. It didn't work.

In Auschwitz reality was so overwhelming, the suffering, the fatigue, the cold so extreme, that we had no energy left for this type of pretending. When I would recite a poem, when I would tell the comrades beside me what a novel or a play was about while we went on digging in the muck of the swamp, it was to keep myself alive, to preserve my memory, to remain me, to make sure of it. Never did that succeed in nullifying the moment I was living through, not for an instant. To think, to remember was a great victory over the horror, but it never lessened it. Reality was right there, killing. There was no possible getting away from it.

How did I manage to extricate myself from it when I returned? What did I do so as to be alive today? People often ask me that question, to which I continue to look for an answer, and still find none.

Auschwitz is so deeply etched in my memory that I cannot forget one moment of it. —So you are living with Auschwitz? —No, I live next to it. Auschwitz is there, unalterable, precise, but enveloped in the skin of memory, an impermeable skin that isolates it from my present self. Unlike the snake's skin, the skin of memory does not renew itself. Oh, it may harden further . . . Alas, I often fear lest it grow thin, crack, and the camp get hold of me again. Thinking about it makes me tremble with apprehension. They claim the dying see their whole life pass before their eyes . . .

In this underlying memory sensations remain intact. No doubt, I am very fortunate in not recognizing myself in the self that was in Auschwitz. To return from there was so improbable that it seems to me I was never there at all. Unlike those whose life came to a halt as they crossed the threshold of return, who since that time survive as ghosts, I feel that the one who was in the camp is not me, is not the person who is here, facing you. No, it is all too incredible. And everything that happened to that other, the Auschwitz one, now has no bearing upon me, does not concern me, so separate from one another are this deep-lying memory and ordinary memory. I live within a twofold being. The Auschwitz double doesn't bother me, doesn't interfere with my life. As though it weren't I at all. Without this split I would not have been able to revive.

The skin enfolding the memory of Auschwitz is tough. Even so it gives way at times, revealing all it contains. Over dreams the conscious will has no power. And in those dreams I see myself, yes, my own self such as I know I was: hardly able to stand on my feet, my throat tight, my heart beating wildly, frozen to the marrow, filthy, skin and bones; the suffering I feel is so unbearable, so identical to the pain endured there, that I feel it physically, I feel it throughout my whole body which becomes a mass of suffering; and I feel death fasten on me, I feel that I am dying. Luckily, in my agony I cry out. My cry wakes me and I emerge from the nightmare, drained. It takes days for everything to get back to normal, for everything to get shoved back inside memory, and for the skin of memory to mend again. I become myself again, the person you know, who can talk to you about Auschwitz without exhibiting or registering any anxiety or emotion.

Because when I talk to you about Auschwitz, it is not from deep memory my words issue. They come from external memory, if I may put it that way, from intellectual memory, the memory connected with thinking processes. Deep memory preserves sensations, physical imprints. It is the memory of the senses. For it isn't words that are swollen with emotional charge.

Otherwise, someone who has been tortured by thirst for weeks on end could never again say "I'm thirsty. How about a cup of tea." This word has also split in two. *Thirst* has turned back into a word for commonplace use. But if I dream of the thirst I suffered in Birkenau, I once again see the person I was, haggard, halfway crazed, near to collapse; I physically feel that real thirst and it is an atrocious nightmare. If, however, you'd like me to talk to you about it . . .

This is why I say today that while knowing perfectly well that it corresponds to the facts, I no longer know if it is real.

She says: "One doesn't die from grief." In her smooth, colorless voice, smooth as her evenly aged face is smooth, as colorless
as her eyes where you occasionally find a glint of their former
blue. "No, it simply isn't so. One doesn't die from grief." In a lower
voice she repeats: "You go on living." You go on living, yes. It's
worse. She lives in her grief, lives with her sorrow, that unalter-
ing double of herself. She bears her grief ever since she bore in
her arms that sister of hers, who died in the night. The night of
all nights whence those who have returned have not issued forth.
She held her dying sister in her arms, hugged her to herself in
order to keep her back, prevent her from slipping out of life.
Softly she blew her breath upon her sister's face to warm the lips
that were turning blue, to impart her own breath to them, and
when her sister's heart stopped, she was filled with anger at her
own which continued to beat. Which yet beats today, after all
these years she has spent on the borders of life. And when she
says that you don't die from grief, she's apologizing for being
alive. Barely alive.

Ever since she carried her sister out into the snow for the
corpse collection squad to pick up and dump on the pile, one
more for the night's pile of bodies, ever since she had loosened
her grip and let go her sister's still faintly warm body that she
had clasped, holding it as tight as she could, sapped as she was
from several weeks of camp, the desperate struggle lasting all
night—; ever since that morning she knows that you don't die
from grief.

Would she be dead had the others not held her upright and got
her to roll-call, kept her from falling into the ditch between the
barracks and the mustering yard, kept her from fainting, held her
on her feet till the end of the roll-call, helped her walk upon the
icy road and reach the marsh, would she be dead? No. That

night she had drawn in her sister's last breath, inside her she bore her sister, alive from now on through her alone.

Like all survivors, she wonders how she returned, and why. The others feel they fought with superhuman determination in order to come back; she doesn't know. She just came back, that's all. Within her heart the whole weight of that night, her inability to share her living breath with her sister, and then the weight of the girl she carried out of the barracks and laid upon the snow, delicately, maternally, a kind of burial, a . . . sacrament of tenderness, before that body became an object to be burned that they shovel onto the pile of last night's dead who will be burned in the course of the day or who, if today there are too many of them, will wait until tomorrow, exposed to the rats.

She came back home, but not back to life. Life flowed over her the way a stream's water flows over the stones it polishes, it wore her away, day by day. Her gaze faded, her voice lost its color, her hair grew gray. How many years now? She counted them, but it's not the right count. Auschwitz was yesterday. That night was last night.

For all these years she has done little things, gone through the little motions of everyday life, she listens to the sounds of the life moving by around her. She hears only the wind blowing across the icy plain, the shouts of the female guards overseeing the prisoners in the frozen marshes, the barking of the dogs. She smells only the smell of the crematorium. She hears the voices of her friends who tore her away from her dead sister's body: "Come on! Come on! We've got to get to roll-call" and who dragged her off, propped her up in the ranks, told her to cry, but she hadn't been able to cry, neither that morning nor since. For lack of tears her gaze has dulled.

What is she holding in her arms
hugged to her breast
that one
in the front row
there, in the row facing ours
yes that one in the front row.
The ranks facing ours
are still Gypsies.
Yes, the Gypsies.
How do you know it's a Gypsy when all that's left of it is a
skeleton?
Since the middle of the night they have been standing
over there in the snow that thousands of feet have trampled
into hardened slippery sheets
Since the middle of the night
we've been here standing in the snow,
standing in the night
the night broken by the spaced floodlights
on the barbed wire fences

IV

The projectors light the barbed wire strung between high white poles. Encircled by light, the camp lies in darkness and in this black abyss nothing can be distinguished nothing except darker shapes swaying ghostlike upon the ice. The roll-call siren has emptied the barracks. By swaying clusters, the women have all stumbled out, clinging to each other so as not to fall
And when one does fall, the whole cluster reels and falls and gets back up, falls again and rises, and in spite of it all moves on. Without a word.

There is only the screaming of the furies who want the barracks to empty faster, want the reeling shades to move faster from the barracks to the space where the roll is called.

In the darkness, for the beams of the projectors do not reach the spaces between the barracks. They light only the gate and the barbed wire enclosure so that the sentinels up in the watchtowers may spot those trying to escape and shoot
as if one could escape
as if one could cut through the fence of high-tension live barbed wire
as if . . .

In the dark you cannot see where you step, you fall into holes, stumble into drifts of snow.

Clutching one another, guided by shouts and blows of clubs, the shades of the night take the places where they must be to await the break of day.

Panic sometimes. Where are you? I'm right here.

Hold on to me, or a voice full of despair: My galoshes. I've lost my galoshes. It's from a woman who slipped, got up, but without her galoshes, flown off who knows in what direction, and the

9

whole group stops, stoops over the snow, gropes unseeingly. The galoshes must be found.

Barefoot at roll-call is certain death. Barefoot in the snow for hours—death.

They're all hunting for the galoshes and others behind them grow impatient and shove because the fury, the barracks leader, in her boots and steady on her feet, comes down on them with her club, screaming as she swings at everyone within reach. In the dark she can't see where she's hitting, the club always strikes someone, lands on those shapes that are squatting and groping and straightening up and, beneath the blows, there fall again those who had succeeded in rising to their feet.

Here, I've got one of them. I've got the other. The galoshes pass from hand to hand until they reach the one they belong to, who murmurs her thanks but is not heard, so exhausted is she by fear, by falls, clubbing, and the hallucinations of the night.

The group sets off again, a chaotic procession. Tortuous wending of its way between obstacles: piles of brick covered with frozen snow, piles of snow, holes full of water turned into ice

a ditch to step over

and the frozen earth, bristling and jagged, like a plowed field petrified into clods of ice.

At last they're all in place, lined up for the roll-call, on each side of the road running down the middle of the camp.

They shall have to wait hours and hours before daybreak, before the counting. The SS do not arrive until it is light.

First you stamp your feet. The cold pierces to the marrow. You no longer feel your body, you no longer feel anything of your self. First you stamp your feet. But it's tiring to stamp your feet. Then you huddle over, arms crossed over your chest, shoulders hunched, and all squeeze close to one another

but keeping in rank because the club-wielding furies are there and watching.

Even the strength to raise one's eyes, to look to see if there are stars in the sky

there's a chilling effect to stars
to cast a glance about
even the strength that takes must be saved and no one looks
up.
And to see what in that darkness?
The women from the other barracks, also reeling and falling,
trying to form their ranks?
all these ranks stretching from one end of the camp to the
other, on each side of the road,
that makes how many women, how many thousands of
women, all these ranks?
these ranks bobbing up and down because the women are
stamping their feet and then they halt because to stamp one's feet
is exhausting
You see nothing, each one is enclosed in the shroud of her own
skin,
you feel nothing, neither the person next to you, huddling
against you, nor that other who has fallen and is being helped
up.
You don't speak because the cold would freeze your saliva.
Each feels she is dying, crumbling into confused images, dead
to herself already, without a past, any reality, without anything,
the sky must have grown light without anyone noticing.
And now, in the pallid light of the night drawing to a close,
the ranks across the way suddenly emerge, the ranks of the
Gypsy women
like ourselves all blue from cold.
How would you know a Gypsy if not by her tattered dress?
The Jewish women do not have striped uniforms either, they
have grotesque clothing, coats too long or too tight, mud-
spattered, torn, with a huge red cross painted on the back.
The Gypsy women have tatters, what's left of their full skirts
and their scarves.
And suddenly there she is, you can make her out, the one
in the front row, holding, clutched to her breast, a bundle of
rags.

In her gaunt face, eyes gleaming so bright that you must look away not to be pierced by them

her eyes gleaming with fever, with hatred, a burning, unbearable hatred.

And what else but hatred is holding together these rags this spectre of a woman is made of, with her bundle pressed against her chest by hands purple from cold?

She holds the bundle of rags to her, in the crook of her arm, the way a baby is held, the baby's head against its mother's breast.

Daylight.

The Gypsy stands straight, so tense that it is visible through her tatters, her left hand placed upon the baby's face. It is an infant, that bundle of rags she is clutching. It became obvious when she shifted the upper part of the bundle, turning it outward a little, to help it breathe perhaps, now that daylight has come.

Quickly she shelters the baby's face again and hugs it tighter then she shifts the bundle of rags to her other arm, and we see the infant's head lolling, bluish, almost black.

With a gentle movement she raises the baby's head, props it in the hollow between her arm and her breast,

and again she lifts her eyes, and again the impression she gives is of tension and fierceness, with her unbearable stare.

The SS arrive. All the women stiffen as they move down the ranks, counting. That lasts a long time. A long time. Finally, one side is done. You can put your hands back in the sleeves of your jacket, you can hunch up your shoulders, as if it were possible to make yourself a smaller target for the cold.

I look at the Gypsy holding her baby pressed against her. It's dead, isn't it?

Yes, it's dead. Its purplish head, almost black, falls back when not supported by the Gypsy's hand.

For how long has it been dead, cradled in its mother's arms, this rag-swaddled infant? For hours, perhaps for days.

The SS move past, counting the ranks of the Gypsies. They do not see the woman with the dead baby and the frightening eyes.

A whistle blows. The roll-call is over. We break formation. Again we slide and fall on the sheet of ice, now spotted here and there with diarrhea.

The Gypsies' formation breaks up too. The woman with the baby runs off. Where is she heading for shelter?

The Gypsies are not marched out of the camp for work. Men, women, children are mixed together in a separate enclosed area. The camp for families. And why are there Gypsy women over here, in our camp? Nobody knows.

When the roll was called that evening she was there, with her dead baby in her arms. Standing in the front row. Standing straight.

The following morning at roll-call she was there, hugging her bundle of rags, her eyes still brighter, still wilder.

Then she stopped coming to roll-call.

Someone saw the bundle of rags, the dead baby, on the garbage heap by the kitchen.

The Gypsy had been clubbed to death by a policewoman who'd tried to pull the dead baby away from her.

This woman, hugging her baby to her, had fought, butting her head, kicking, protecting herself and then striking with her free hand ... a struggle in which she had been crushed despite the hate that gave her the strength of a lioness defending her brood.

The Gypsy had fallen dead in the snow. The corpse collection squad had picked up her body and carried it to where the corpses are stacked before being loaded on the truck which dumps them at the crematorium.

The mother killed, the policewoman had torn the baby from her arms and tossed it on the garbage heap in front of which the struggle had taken place. The Gypsy woman had raced to the edge of the camp, tightly cradling the baby in her crossed arms, had run till she was out of breath and it was when she was blocked by the garbage pile that she turned to face the fury and her club.

The corpse collection squad picked up the mother. The baby, in its rags, remained on the garbage heap, mixed with the refuse.

13

All the Gypsies disappeared very fast. All gassed. Thousands of them. The family camp was emptied out, that made room for the next arrivals. Not Gypsies. We saw nothing more of Gypsies at Birkenau. Gypsies are less numerous than Jews, it didn't take much time to dispose of them.

V

My mother, the stars

The whole while that you were there
that I didn't know where you were
I never closed my bedroom shutters
at night
I never drew the curtains.
From my bed
I would look at a star,
always the same star.
The minute it appeared
I'd recognize it.
I kept thinking
Charlotte too is looking at the sky
She too sees that star.
Wherever she is, she sees it.
She knows that I think of her
that I'm thinking of her every minute
every second
I didn't want to go to sleep
for fear my thoughts toward you would slumber.
I'd fall asleep in the morning
when daylight erased my star.
On the nights the sky was covered
I'd follow the shifting clouds
so as not to miss my star
when it emerged
from a break in the clouds.
To see it
just for a minute
to see it.
It told me you were alive.

I didn't like starless nights
nor full moon nights
when glowing moonlight devoured the stars.
It seemed to me I was losing sight of you.

Now that you are back
I'll close the shutters.
They must be very rusty.

During all that while, that long while

My mother never again talked to me about the camp, never
asked me anything about Auschwitz.

VI

What killed me was to find out my mother had not been gassed.

For everybody, gassing was the worst—a terrifying image, scenes of horror. Not for me. I don't know how to put it to you. I mean I feel it differently. When I was arrested I didn't feel afraid. My mother had been deported six months before. We knew she had been sent off. She had tossed a note from the train, we got it. I hadn't had any further news from her, of course. I spent only three days in Drancy. Then right away the cattle-car. Destination unknown. Who had even heard the name of Auschwitz? With me, in the packed cattle-car, women and children. The children yelled or moaned. The women cried silently. Three nights, three days without a drop of water to wash the babies, nothing for the bottles, dry bread for the bigger ones. The women cried quietly, without stirring, keeping a tender, reassuring hand on their children. They had no idea what would become of them, of the little ones. They were frightened. I wasn't. I took it easy, I was almost happy: I was going to see Mama again. It didn't occur to me that the convoys leaving Drancy might be sent to several places. I assumed they were putting all the Jews in the same place. Mama was there already, I was going to join her. It was as simple as that to my girlish mind. The funny part was that I was right. From France, the Jews were dispatched to Auschwitz. They all got on my nerves, those women who moaned or else sat in a daze. The men were in another car. At every stop everyone shouted family or first names to find out how the others were doing. I thought to myself that judging from the way they treated us from the start, we obviously couldn't expect anything good to happen. Well, so what? We'll see by and by. The vitality you have when you're fifteen!

I held on to the food I had been given for the trip. Good stuff from the country: honey, pâté, packed by my nurse. I kept it all for Mama.

Getting down out of the train, on the ballast, shouts, dogs, boots, guns. You remember that too, but when I got there it wasn't the middle of winter, it wasn't so awful. Besides, my heart was so full of joy. To see Mama again. Together we'd overcome any hardship. The journey hadn't tired me that much. I had just turned fifteen, strong as a little ox. I had the apple cheeks of the country girl I had become during the two years I'd been with the farm woman my parents had entrusted me to for safekeeping. Alert, eyes open, I observed, I watched—as if I'd had eyes on all sides of my head. Nothing escaped me and I ducked the blows almost automatically. At the sight of the dogs the others backed off right into the clubs; as for me, I slipped off to the side. I must say that I wasn't weighted down by anything. The others had their kids. All I had was my small bundle.

When they ordered the women with children and the old people to line up on one side—I understood because German is a lot like Yiddish—I said to myself—and it came to me like that, quick as lightning—"Oh no, I'm not going to line up with these whining women and their kids. Not with the old folks either. And end up in some kind of nursing home, emptying chamberpots—not me!" When they called the bigger children I didn't budge either. I stuck out my chest, already round, and stood up tall. If I wanted to be with Mama I had to line up with the women. That's how I made it to Birkenau. There, of course, it was really something. The corpses, the stench, the rot. Still, there were women in striped dresses going this way and that. So, those who had entered the camp had not all died. My mother would be among them. I refused to see any of the horror. I kept my eyes wide open, I stared at every woman prisoner who went by. Even dressed that way, even with her head shaved, even limping, I'd recognize Mama if I saw her.

They put us into an already overcrowded barracks. Except for our small group there was no one French. Slovaks, Hungarians.

I questioned eveyone I could. Nobody had seen Mama. In six months the camp population had turned over completely, as you know. But Mama was strong. With all these barracks, how was I to find her? I'd have to go everywhere, and so as soon as I could, that evening after the roll-call, I ran about from one barracks to the next. They didn't even answer me. A tall blond woman, with beautiful gray eyes. As if there were still blonds and gray eyes in any such place as that.

It wasn't until at least two weeks after we got there that I heard talk about gas chambers. I didn't believe it, of course. Famished, worn out, in bad shape as they all were, these women weren't in their right minds. Who can believe such a horror story? At the same time, I wondered where all those who had lined up along the tracks had gone to. I tried reasonable answers to my questions: the aged were in a nursing home, the babes in arms and their mothers in a . . . in a what? And the bigger children, the ones under fourteen or fifteen who had been called to one side? To go on from there to supposing they'd been asphyxiated in a gas chamber . . . Hundreds of them? Impossible. Finally I had to face the truth. A couple of hundred people were plainly dying in the camp every day, but the smoke constantly coming from those enormous smokestacks, the odor of burned flesh . . . But these trains we saw arrive in the morning as we were starting out to work; and yet on certain days not a single new face in the camp. The work column would halt and mark time while they formed into ranks. These thousands of people . . . who arrived every day, without the camp population getting any larger. You could check it by the tattooed numbers. And those lines waiting in front of a little door, that you never saw come out again . . . One day we'd been working close. They'd gone in all day long. Women patting the little ones to keep them quiet, the bigger ones well behaved, with serious faces like children who don't want to be treated like babies. Old people, barely able to keep on their feet, and others too, not all that old, as I think of them today. The door opened only when the line was long enough to make a complete batch. Just the way you wait to have enough dirty clothes to make a load for the machine. Showers? You don't take a shower packed together as in the subway at rush hour. So when a Czech woman who worked with the clothes—you know, the team that sorted out and stacked what the people took off in order to go naked into the gas chamber—, when that Czech woman explained the system to me, I told myself that my mother, maybe because she was carrying a baby for someone who had several of them, or perhaps because she was helping some old lady having trouble walking, I told myself that my mother had got herself into the wrong line and that she'd been gassed.

You won't believe it, but I felt relieved. By then I had become acquainted with life and death in the camp. I was filthy, in rags, covered with lice, a stinking scarecrow. I was at the end of my rope. At least Mama wouldn't have had to endure that. She'd been spared this degradation.

Following my return I adjusted myself to that idea, a comforting one all told. I see you don't understand. For you the worst of all is the gas chamber, isn't it?

Well, recently . . . You know they've found the lists of those in all the shipments that left from Drancy, and they even know what happened to those shipments. Well, I recently learned that for the convoy my mother was in—her name is there on the list—there was no selection upon arrival, no special line for the young and the old. An exceptional case, you can call it that. The whole shipment went into the camp. Perhaps their stock of gas had run out.

She had tried to make a joke. There was a pause in her voice as she repressed a sob.

"Your mother died almost forty years ago. Why do you torture yourself? Gassed or not gassed—what difference does that make?"

I had spoken too quickly. I recall that in my prison cell, where we were several women with husbands who were or who would be condemned to death, one of us said, "Me, I would prefer the guillotine. It's cleaner, quicker. I'm sure you suffer less." And I had a picture of the severed head, its eyes rolled back. I shivered with horror and my heart climbed up into my mouth. Beheaded, shot—these young men not yet in their thirties. And even so, I thought, the guillotine is worse than bullets in the chest. My husband was shot.

She went on. You don't understand, she said, you don't understand that that changes everything. When I was positive that my mother had been gassed without entering the camp, I was less unhappy. I could put up with everything, telling myself that Mama had not witnessed this, had not undergone this. She died without realizing what this place was. She'd been told to undress, and five minutes later it was over with. She entered the gas chamber the way we went into the showers when we arrived. You remember. When they told us to get undressed we got undressed without suspecting anything wrong. All I was worried about was not losing my little package of food. I had to turn it in along with my clothing. Oh, how that hurt! When they ordered us into the showers we went in there without seeing anything odd about it. It was a real shower. Fine. So, for Mama . . . for Mama it was gas; but she didn't know it. That's what I said to myself and I felt almost reassured.

But no, she wasn't that lucky. Today, the full horror of Birkenau comes back to me through my mother. I'd forgotten. No, that's not the right word. You can't forget anything. I mean I had just stopped thinking about it. No, I was able to think about it without it hurting. Sometimes a nightmare, otherwise nothing painful.

When I returned I was seventeen. My mother had died without having had time to suffer, believing I was safe. I wanted to live. Life is strong in you at seventeen. And now, the truth.

I wonder now how she died. And when. How long she suffered. I've tried without success to locate women in her convoy. Not one survivor. I would have seen them in the camp had they held on until my arrival. If you knew how I searched for her there! Everything pointed to my mother having been gassed with her whole convoy. Since that isn't so, I wonder how long Mama held on. Perhaps she died on the eve of my arrival. How long did she suffer? She wasn't forty—but for Birkenau that's old. But she was so brave. And strengthened by the longing to see her children again, above all me, whom she had had to leave so young. I am the last-born. I am sure she fought to the last drop of her strength. And you know how far that last drop could take those who wanted to get back. Today, it all comes back to me in visions of Mama in its midst. Is it my mother, that woman a dog drags for thirty feet over a stony road and then leaves there, her throat torn open, moaning, then ceasing to moan? Or this other one, unable to get up under the beating she is receiving? The SS go on bludgeoning an already lifeless rag. Or is she one of these skeleton-like typhus cases in a group being removed from the infirmary to Block 25? Or one of the corpses piling up in the mud? And if she died in the infirmary, stark naked, covered with lice, her skin scraped by the rough boards of the bunks, with the rats busy all around? Mama . . . She dragged herself to the swamp, exhausted by dysentery, and nasty, stinking, she who used to be so fastidious. There is no end to all those atrocious images. I don't need to remind you of all the ways there were to die in Birkenau, every one of them atrocious. The one thing I am sure of is that she didn't take her own life, didn't end it by throwing herself onto the electrified barbed wire. She was far too tenacious for that.

Now I'll never know. Indeed, even if I came across someone who was with her, I wouldn't be told the truth. Have you told the truth to the kin of those who died back there? Without passing the word along, all the survivors have said the same thing: he or she died of typhus. In a coma, without suffering. So as not to cause pain to the members of the family, at least so as not to worsen it.

No, I won't ever know.

"Come, you mustn't go on torturing yourself. What does it matter today? Time has healed the wounds."

And it's you who say such a thing? You? You don't understand. I lived with the idea my mother had died without suffering. Sure, I grieved for her. It's always terrible to lose one's mother. That pain, yes, time had lessened it. But today the wound opens again and it hurts all the more because the scar had hardened.

VII

No, I'm not sorry I was sent there. I'm even rather glad I was. That seems odd to you? You're going to understand. No, I'm not the guy who comes back proud of having lived through something unusual. There's none of that stuff be ween you and me. You know that I was arrested a first time along with my mother. I haven't told you about that? It was one of the first big roundups, in '42. One day there's a rumor going around: a roundup of Jews, for tomorrow or the day after. Where did the rumor originate? Perhaps from central headquarters of the Paris police. I'm just trying to save its honor . . . In our house we never altogether believed it. We weren't living in the Jewish neighborhood: rue des Rosiers, rue des Ecouffes, the Temple. We lived near the Bastille. My mother had persuaded my father to leave the house and hide out somewhere at least long enough for things to blow over. He left without saying where he was going. For at the beginning it was thought they only took the men. Women and children weren't supposed to be in any danger. I stayed with my mother, listening, on the look out. Nothing. And the following day the cops came to pick us up. Who had tipped them off? Even today I've no idea. My mother got some things together, pretty much haphazardly, and put them in a big shopping bag. She wanted to empty the larder. "That'll do it, let's get going!" A bus, an ordinary green bus, public transportation, with its open back platform was waiting down there, already crowded. We found our way to some vacant seats inside. Nobody looked at anybody else, each pretending he was there through some mistake. There were old people, young people, women, children. All aboard! We drive through Paris and wind up in front of the Vel d'Hiv. Other buses crammed with people were arriving at the same time. You had to wait in line to get in. We got in line, my mother and I. I didn't fuss—I was fourteen and acting like a little man. My mother was calm, didn't say a word. I didn't notice that she was watching everything going on around us. Suddenly, without turning my way, she whispered: "Get out of here. Take this"—a light wool vest she had over her arm, something she'd grabbed at the last minute: you know, in the middle of the summer, she'd thought of something for the cool evenings—"hold it in front of you to hide your star. Go along quietly. Don't look back, don't run. Goodbye. Now go!" I slipped out of the line, just where my mother had noticed a gap between the cops. I tried to look natural. After a couple of blocks I couldn't prevent myself from running. Then I asked myself where I was running to. I slowed down. My mother had told me to go along quietly. Go where? Not home, obviously. Not to the homes of relatives or Jewish friends. It seemed to me all of a sudden that I didn't know anyone. I walked through the streets. As evening was falling I knocked on the door of a school friend— it was the only place that finally occurred to me. His parents— they weren't Jews—invited me right in. I told them what had happened. They fed me. I was dying of hunger. They fixed a cot for me in my friend's room.

"The next day I tore off my star. I didn't go back to school. I looked for my father. Meanwhile he had been looking for us, but it took over a week before we found one another. Thank heavens. I was beginning to feel embarrassed about taking advantage of my friend's hospitality. At fourteen I had done enough standing in line in front of empty shops to know what it meant to have an extra mouth to feed. My father, who had thought things over since leaving us to go into hiding, had a clear view of the situation. "What we're not going to do," he said to me, "is hide like scared rabbits waiting for all of us to be caught before doing something. If we've got to hide, very well, let it be for a purpose."

I went by my friend's house to thank his parents, especially his mother who'd been so warm to me. With my friend I took on a knowing and mysterious air, hinting that I was joining an organization.

26

I hid out with my father. It wasn't long, though, before he made the contacts that would get us across the demarcation line, and we joined up with a resistance group that was then forming. There it was easier. The guys had everything set up for ration cards, forged papers, hideouts. At first it was propagandizing in town. Then a *maquis* took shape: sabotage, attacks on German soldiers, radio liaison with London. On the whole it worked well. And I had the impression we were going to pull through, that the end of the war was approaching—and then I was captured with several others in my group. That was in the Spring of '44. The Gestapo identified me in no time. It was the classic itinerary: Drancy, Auschwitz. No, I was forgetting: the guys who were captured with me, being adults, were shot. I was sixteen years old.

At Auschwitz the system had reached perfection. The gas chambers were running round the clock. Naturally, we—the passengers in my cattle-car—knew nothing of their existence and the selection upon our arrival didn't frighten us. Moreover, nothing frightened me anymore. In the Spring of '44 Hitler had lost the war. It was only a question of a few months.

Big for my age, I was put into the column of able-bodied men which marched into the camp. The others were marched to the showers—as I found out a few weeks afterwards. You're not someone who needs to be told how it was, what I endured—the standard experience.

In the men's camp it was difficult if not impossible to communicate with Birkenau, the women's camp. My mother must have been there at some time. When we passed the women's columns, on the way to the marshes, the idea that my mother could have held out for two years simply struck me as ridiculous. She was surely already dead. I never managed to find out anything at all about her.

"And later, when you got home?"

"I didn't expect my mother to come back. No, I had no hope, not even a subconscious one, of her return. To hold out in Birkenau from July of '42 until '45—it would have been a miracle. We were terrible realists in my family, you remember. I don't know how my mother died. I left it at that."

"And your father?"

"He came through the whole business. Talk about luck! Incredible."

"He didn't try to find out, like just about everyone else?"

"No. I told him what the situation had been, as briefly as possible. We didn't much enjoy talking when we got back. I think he understood right away. He hasn't inquired."

"Even now with what they know about the destinations of the convoys?"

"When I said that I was rather glad to have been there, it's—how should I put it? Anyhow, you surely know what I mean, you of all people. For me, my mother didn't just vanish into some black hole, she wasn't just gobbled up into nothingness, some unimaginable place you can piece together from the accounts of survivors. I know what my mother went through, what she saw, what she suffered, and it's something I feel I shared with her."

VIII

I too
would look at the stars
During the calling of the roll
at night
long before daybreak
shards of icy diamonds
incandescent stings
diamonds of ice
arrows of fire
perforating the metal of the sky
to plant in our flesh
their splinters of cold
their burning
sharp claws
stabbing us to the heart.
Indifferent their light
their cruelty
was it so
uncaring
deadly
as everything
here
the snow paralyzing our feet
snow
its cold gripping our temples
the wind with its cutting blades
the night with its crystal needles

Everyone
thousands
outside in the night
standing in the cold of the night

blue from cold
chests so tightened it hurts
indifferent to pain
indifferent to death
locking us in its icy grip.
And it's morning's night
yet another whole day to come
to live through till end of day
till evening's night.

Under the stars' dismayed stare
a line from a poem rose
within my dismayed memory
to figure this implacable hardness.
Yet the line pleased me
and I spoke it again
as if to entreat the stars
begging them to soften their stare.

When I returned I reread the poems of Blaise Cendrars
and failed to find the line which had surfaced
transformed
within the memory
belonging to me
there.

IX

This time it was true. I was back in my own country. Just when I had stopped believing it could ever happen, so unbridgeable was the gulf separating me from my homeland, I had returned. Spanish was being spoken all around me. Men's voices. What sort of place was this? A café probably. I didn't ask through what series of circumstances I had landed in a café, a place where I had never set foot before. It was warm in there. The air was thick with smoke. The smell of tobacco, the smell of a fire burning, the smell of men. Nothing but men's voices. What a fine dream! Oh yes, I often think about my country, I think about it all the time, but I rarely dream about it. What brings on dreams? If I knew I'd always summon this one: being in Spain, hearing Spanish spoken.

Apparently with the intention of having me take part in their feast, a man came over to me, raised my head—I felt the rough fabric of his sleeve on the nape of my neck—and said, speaking with a Castilian accent: "Drink, my little dove," and he made me sip some wine from a metal cup. I didn't see his face. How long it had been since I had drunk any wine! It was good wine. It was warming. "Another little nip?" My senses began to reawaken. Gradually. I made no effort to come out of my dream. I wanted to stay in it forever. However, my eyes were opening. I looked around, trying to figure out where I was.

In my dream, it was all coherent, clear. With my eyes open, it was all fantastic, inexplicable. The man was there all right, a Spaniard with a Castilian accent, and he was holding my head up and helping me drink: "A little more?" "No more, thank you," I replied in Spanish, "that's enough." Astonished, the man straightened up. "She's Spanish! Did you hear that? A Spanish girl!" he shouted to those in the adjoining room. They all came in and crowded around me. I was stretched out upon a bench, with some rolled up clothing for a pillow and a blanket over my legs. "A Spanish girl here? How'd she get here?" "Hey, are you really Spanish? Where are you from?"

I couldn't figure out where I was. It was all unreal. I tried to recall the circumstances that had preceded my waking up in this unknown house, amidst these Spanish soldiers. Yes, they were soldiers. They wore a uniform, a uniform I was not familiar with. How had I got to this place? I couldn't remember and I floated as if in a continuing dream. Curious, they asked me more and more questions. Little by little the questions were helping to bring back my memory, but what I was saying was so unrelated to these men, this house, the fire crackling in a great big stove. The kind of stove they have here, tiled. I couldn't make things fit together, and what I was saying didn't seem real.

"You say you're from Bilbao. So how did you ever get to this godforsaken country? Were you kidnapped?"

"No, I taught school in Bilbao."

"School?" They didn't understand. I started off on a long story, but no, here's the gist of it: 1937, the Civil War, Bilbao surrounded by Franco's troops, Bilbao ready to fall under their fire. The children have to be evacuated, saved from the bombings. The children are put aboard fishing boats, with some teachers, single women, therefore the younger ones. I in the midst of my little girls, waving goodbye to Bilbao while the boat sets sail for Leningrad. We get to Leningrad, the children are settled in some old buildings converted into dormitories, and the teachers organize classes given in Spanish. They're to go back to Spain when the war is over, once the Republicans have won.

"We'll take those children away from the Bolsheviks and bring them back to Spain," one of the men said.

"So, these kids, you were their teacher."

"Later I married a Russian, an engineer. When Hitler invaded Russia my husband was drafted from his factory in Leningrad and then to the front in Byelorussia."

"How did you manage so that our patrol picked you up here half frozen in the snow?"

"In the snow? Frozen?" It was becoming confused again.
"Yes, this guy over here brought you back to life, rubbed your feet. Can you feel them now? Have a little more wine?"

"When I found out my husband had been killed—it happened two or three days after he joined his unit—I decided to get to Moscow. I'm four months pregnant. I wanted to be with my in-laws when the baby came. The front was moving close to Leningrad. It was the same as in Bilbao. I could tell that soon no one would get out.

"Well, lady, it's a real coincidence. We're heading for Moscow too. We'll get there before you do—but don't tell me you were figuring on hoofing it all the way to Moscow?"

"On account of being pregnant I got a seat on a train. The tracks were bombed out. The train stopped. We spent all night in the cars, without light or heat. Even though there were a lot of us crowded together, it really got very cold. Some passengers went out to try to find out what was happening, when we'd start again. I got out too and started walking towards a village which didn't look so very far away. I walked for as long as I could. I remember now that I dropped with exhaustion, then I got up again."

"Then you fell down again. Well, little Republic, we've taken you prisoner."

They said that nicely, grinning and delighted with their find: a Spanish girl pulled out of the snow of the Russian plain.

"What's your name?"

"Nieves."

"Nieves, did you hear that? Snow! Well, you can say Our Lady of the Snows has got some clout around here. Your patron saint must have a close eye on you to have steered us to you in the middle of this nowhere."

"And you? How come all of you are here?"

"We're the Blue Division. We're on our way to save the world from Bolshevism."

I'd had no idea there was a Spanish contingent on the Russian front. They were all volunteers, they added proudly. It was some company I'd landed in. The fog in my brain was beginning to lift, but there were things I still didn't understand.

"Where are we?"

"In a Baltic village. In the house of people who took off. Fortunately they left plenty of firewood. There's enough to heat the place night and day. So you'll just stay here with us and get well. You'll be our mascot prisoner."

To have come all the way from Bilbao only to find myself in the hands of Falangists! I wasn't afraid of them, they were very friendly, but I didn't know how to interpret what they were saying.

"We're not going to chase you out of here in weather like this. You're not going to reach Moscow on foot. And get through the German lines? Rest up here while we figure out what to do with you."

And so they kept me there. They were nice to me. Decent guys, polite. They watched their language when I was around. They weren't at all the bloodthirsty brutes we feared in Bilbao. People change with changing circumstances. In the morning they made themselves cocoa with condensed milk and gave me some. Something whose taste I'd forgotten about long ago, in Leningrad.

A woman quartered with soldiers, not at all according to regulations; but in the field, as they told me, it's the highest ranking officer who makes the rules.

When they received the order to move out, two of them took me to the *Kommandantur* and explained my case. We were sorry to say goodbye. They gave me some of their rations, kissed me right in front of the German officer—this was beyond him—and wished me good luck: "Next year in Bilbao! Right?"

The *Kommandantur* captain was less naive. No nonsense with him. He turned me straight over to a Gestapo man who didn't believe one bit of my story. He beat me and beat me to make me admit I was a spy whose job was to reconnoiter the positions of the Blue Division. Despite the exact details I gave to bear out my story, he'd have none of it. I was thrown into the Riga prison. That's where I gave birth. The baby was stillborn.

34

The Riga prison was overcrowded. Balts, Russians, truckloads of them arrived every day. When the place was really too full the order came to transfer the women to Ravensbrück where, after a journey in a cattle-car lasting several days—for there were constant stops on sidings to allow troop trains to pass on their way to the front—I found myself in a barracks amidst Russians. But in April 1945, when they called the French women forward to set them free, I joined their ranks. I wanted to go to France. There was nothing to keep me in Russia anymore. I knew no one in France, but it is next door to Spain. Since the war was over, I'd go back home. Mussolini and Hitler were dead, Franco had to be also. Victory had crushed all the tyrants. Such was my fond belief.

In Paris, at the rest and recuperation center, I met Spaniards coming back from Mauthausen. They were Republican combatants who after the defeat had taken refuge in France and had been interned in French camps at the foot of the Pyrenees. Handed over to the Germans after the June 1940 armistice, they had been deported to Mauthausen. More than three out of four had succumbed in the Mauthausen quarries. And what a state the survivors were in. Far worse off than us, the women from Ravensbrück.

They made me a part of their group at once. Their next stop was Toulouse; I went with them. Continue on into Spain? When would it be possible to return there? Franco was still in power.

In Toulouse life wasn't easy at first. Fortunately there was a colony of Republicans and they all helped each other out. I married a Spaniard, an Andalusian. We have two children. They're big now. They've never seen Spain.

I often wonder what happened to my Bilbao schoolgirls. Some had returned in 1953, at the same time as some Blue Division survivors whom the Russians had held prisoner for nearly ten years. Others remained in the Soviet Union, marrying and settling there.

To return home! So strong had been that wish that we had always refused to tie ourselves down in France, say by buying a house or an apartment. At the consulate I was told I could go to Bilbao and in 1969, when the right was extended, all the Spanish refugees were able to return, but my husband had sworn never to set foot on Spanish soil while Franco ruled. We waited, we hoped, we yearned for that jackal's death. And when he was dying what a long time he took to do it. Hearing he was sick, we were at first thrilled. It is an awful thing to wish for a man to die, yes it is. But was that a man? Finally he's going to croak! The days went by, he was still breathing, and our joy lost its edge.

I don't know how he was able to live for so long with all the hatred that had accumulated on his head. He took his own good time to die. The knives ready to be plunged into his heart fell from our fists: nothing would avenge those we had lost. How much misery, how many bereavements, how many ruined lives! An entire nation bent under tyranny or condemned to exile, and those desperate revolts which had always been crushed, those long lists of death sentences, long after the war had ended.

Now that we are in a position to go back, we are old. Our parents are dead, our friends have disappeared. To be sure, we still have ties back there. In our country, family ties extend a long way, through generations of cousins. But our children are as French as they are Spanish. My eldest son married a girl from Toulouse, a good looking woman, with hair as dark as any Spaniard's.

We go there on holidays. A few days in the Basque country, where I am from, a few days in Andalusia, where my husband has his people. Everyone says "Stay! Stay!" It's a temptation. Perhaps we'll buy a house for our retirement. I'd prefer the Basque country. I like being on the shore. And then the Basques were for the Republic from the start, while Andalusia . . . The children would come to visit . . . We still haven't decided anything. We are exiles from everywhere, strangers everywhere.

X

TOMB OF THE DICTATOR

Death's purveyor
long her foremost supplier
gorging her with lives of his choosing
ravaged hopes, sacrificial youth,
exciting her already avid greed,
and giving unto her
giving yet more unto her
and more and still more and more than her fill,
sating the insatiable whom
he at the same time entices
with fodder forever fresher;
flattering the hag
and why?
To fend her off, for he is afraid.
He is afraid and to divert her from himself
daily he dispatches her to the farthest corners of the land.
Has he not spoiled her beyond measure
and will she not keep him immortal?
Why of course! The absolute is immortal
Hence absolute power, and the eternal tyrant too.
Death's master, he thinks he is master over his life
when the thankless one turns his way.
He feels her claws upon his neck
he hears her laughter,
he would loosen those claws
silence the iron castanets
and to quiet her gives her five more men,
among the bravest and most ardent,
alive through and through,
five at a go, one morning in autumn.

Transparent mornings, glowing autumn golden mists.
—And now will you let me live.
No one will ever serve you better.
Five proud men in their prime,
is there any richer feast?
Will she ever be sated?
No, it's him, him she wants.
—Let me go. Let me go.
There are still so many
So many I can give you, wait.
The submissive mistress has turned rebellious.
Her claws sink into his neck.
He gasps, struggles. In vain.
He struggles
and while he agonizes
there is no response to his cries
but sneers, and wagers how long he will last
so terrible is the hatred
that has heaped upon him.
Bloodthirsty in the exact sense
—where is the blood he has fed on for years?
into his shrunken veins, burst pipes,
liters and liters of borrowed blood's to be poured
and this blood decanted into him
fails to fill his flaccid veins, full of holes and
which lose it from a thousand irreparable leaks.
Did he then not shed all the blood on earth
that some still be found to restore movement to this petrified
heart?

Though of stone, had he then a heart?
And as blood does not suffice
they carry in the saint of the miraculous mantle
one whose mantle never shielded an innocent.
Didn't she know, this saint,
that the tyrant's condemned
were condemned unjustly? As if saints knew anything

of human rights.
They resort to every device
summon aid from every quarter
saints, crucifixes, amulets
every manner of wonder-working relic.
—And his relics, the relics of him,
those pieces removed from his carcass,
those relics,
will they erect basilicas for them?
They cut morsels from him, casting them to Death
So that she be patient a while longer.
—One little moment! Let me settle my business
says the widow.

Death keeps tight hold
and it gladdens me.
—You're not ashamed?
—Ashamed? I? And he?
What respect did he ever show for life, happiness, love,
did he ever acknowledge the beauty,
the life in the heart of a young man,
on the lips of a girl?
Power is the power of death.
To be absolute, the reign must be over a graveyard,
corpses are mute and docile.
So death to all who breathe freely!
—Is not every dying man entitled to respect?
—No. Not every one. Not he.
Those who
in the bowels of prisons, in the dark of dungeons,
to whom of an evening
a guard announced by the dread rattling of his keys
has come to say
"It's for tomorrow morning,"
who have agonized solitary and lucid,
those yes, but not he.

The tyrant who lives out his span, after everything
—after all his crimes—
will he ever pay for those other agonies?
Now he's agonizing
an unending leave-taking
and to loosen death's grip
to it he gives up piece by piece strips of his body
beginning with the rottenest.

—Even rotten, he still had guts, did he not?
The tyrant's dying.
No pitying sigh arises from anyone's lips
no sign of regret in anyone's eyes.
—Let him croak! Let him croak!
And the sooner the better!
Let him croak!
During a turn for the better he might
sign further death warrants.
So long as there's breath in his body
even if it means guiding his icy hand
over the slick paper
he'll kill.
So long as he's not quite dead
he can still sign.
May he croak! Think of the comrades
who, at nightfall,
listen for the sound of the keys
their death-knell advancing from down the hall.

—No! May he last and endure!
Behind closed eyelids may he see
the firm features of those he has assassinated.
May he see his victims' unbearable stare,
may he see eternity in that infant's eyes
one hand clinging to its mother's breast
in front of the church at Badajoz

the only living being in the corpse-strewn square.
May he see once more Guernica's tattered flesh
and the men of Burgos
dying from cold in their cells!
May he see it all and be afraid
May a hyena devour his eyes
while sight is yet in them
and may he see his own eyes in the eyes of the beast.
May he undergo a thousand deaths
and thousands more
as many as he inflicted.
All that will hardly console us for having no hand in it
for having failed to reach him with the knives we sharpened
for having failed to avenge our friends and kin,
for not having shortened the time of this infamy
there being nothing that can console us
free us of remorse
for not having avenged our dead.

Sharpening knives . . .
In the high-vaulted space where the tyrant is dying,
between the pillars of the lofty hall,
they are all there,
his heirs
sleepless from dread of losing their place,
all there,
daggers bared,
with one hand each protecting his throat from the blades of
                                                    the others
with the other gripping tight his weapon
to cut a rival throat before his own is cut.
And beneath the high vaults where the tyrant is dying
between the pillars
shadows glide and wait
to make their claim and confront each other.
Gliding shadows and flashes of steel

crossing and disengaging
parrying and pursuing each other
through the deadly maze where destiny lies.

Concealed behind thick veils, her ferocity
hidden behind dark veils, her dry eyes, her pinched lips
the widow keeps steady watch over the dying man.
She does not only watch, she gives orders
Let the tyrant be kept alive
postpone his agony
fabricate his seeming survival
until she's had time to ensure her future and her clan's.
They're all there in the high-ceilinged chamber
features strained behind their masks
masks the tyrant's death will snatch away
this unending agony concluding.
All there
as fearful of one another
as of the people
awaiting the end of the dying
to let forth their joy, their cries
shouting: justice!
shouting: liberty!
shouting: truth!
The heirs tremble.
Are the tyrant's crimes part of the inheritance
and shall the heirs be taxed therefor?
He alone had the power to inflict death
lacking that power the widow buys time
with this interminable agony
they take the suitable steps
fill the prisons with enemies, real or supposed.
—Real, rest assured,
the only truth of tyranny is
that its friends are false, its enemies real.
The heirs dispatch their henchmen to the farthest provinces

impatient to have the right to sign death warrants
themselves.

After all that endless dying
the butcher of his people
stored in the cooler like meat at the butcher's
is finally dead.
And the prelate who'd lent it to him
will come to claim the arm of Saint Theresa
a bone in a golden case
the tyrant kept by him.
You're never protected enough.
The lives of tyrants are always in danger.
Saint Theresa, what have you done?

Grotesque macabre
worthy of him
this end.

XI

My hospital had been almost entirely requisitioned by the German army. Reserved for the gravely wounded, it was chock-full. We were exhausted; we did what we could. There were often periods of several weeks when I couldn't get home to sleep. I'd take a nap on a cot, at the back of one of the wards. The wounded came from every direction. In 1942, Vienna was still well away from the front. The poor creatures got to us after an interminable journey. In war time, the hospital trains have no special priority. They arrived in an appalling state. War. The director calls me in one day. "We're opening a new service, you'll be in charge of it."

"A new service? Where? Where on earth will you put it? We don't have a square foot left in the corridors."

"I'm having this building cleared," and he points to it on the floor plan tacked to the wall behind his chair. It was a place I'd never set foot in. "You'll see—it's a bit . . . well, I'm giving you two teams of cleaners. Get to it right away. The wounded are coming in the day after tomorrow."

I dash off to have a look at my new service. At the far end of the last courtyard I see a run-down building that has been used as a dumping space for castoffs. A tangle of dismantled beds, rusty chairs, old sterilizers, various bits of equipment difficult to identify in the mess. Spiderwebs everywhere, broken window-panes. And only two days to have everything ready? Patients in a place like this? The cleaning women show up, begin by carrying out all that rubbish and piling it along the wall outside. Once the room is empty they begin to wash and scrub. They are at it till late at night. In the morning it looked almost done. An electrician was to put in some lights. We'd have to wait for plumbing. There was a spigot in the courtyard. Toilets?

The director comes in to inspect this new annex. "Your patients are on the way. I guess you're ready."

"Nothing's ready. Just look around. It's clean, but that's all."

"But that's fine."

"How many patients?"

"Around forty."

"And how many nurses are you giving me?"

"You know very well I don't have any nurses," he whined. "I've got some nurse's aides, I'm giving you two. But you'll have no trouble managing, you'll see."

"Forty patients? There's barely room for fifteen beds in here."

"Don't you worry, it's all going to work out. There's a war going on, you mustn't expect too much . . ." and he gives me a sad glance.

The supply officer from whom I request beds tells me he has no requisition for beds.

"Well, straw mattresses then—you can't expect me to put my patients on the bare floor."

"All right," he says, "all right, I'll take care of it."

I collect pails from here and there, wash-basins, a couple of stools. I draw up a list of the linen I'll need, and go running in search of what I consider the absolute minimum.

In the afternoon three military vans, red crosses painted on their roofs, pull up in front of my building. Two soldiers carry out laundry baskets, you know, the kind of wicker baskets laundresses use for storing clean, folded laundry ready for ironing. The soldiers carry the baskets carefully—they're old soldiers, from the territorial reserves—and set them down gently at the door. The weather was chilly, but not raining. A faintly perceptible life stirred in the baskets. Of course, I say to myself. How silly of me. Those are infants they've evacuated from a bombed nursery. Why didn't anyone tell me? Babies in baskets—not very convenient for caring for babies, but it's a sensible way of transporting them. They'd be snugly held inside.

I step up, and instantly recoil. Those weren't babies; those were men's heads. Yes, heads of men, ill-shaven men, with living

46

eyes, heads without bodies. Was it possible? I thought I was hallucinating.

The old soldiers carried the baskets into the ward, asking me where I wanted them placed. All those wide-open, feverish eyes looking out of enormous bodyless heads. A stretcher-bearer murmurs to me: "Blown up by mines. Haven't any more arms or legs."

"What, all of them at the same time?"

"They come from a number of places. They're grouping them here. Got to put them somewhere."

It was taking the stuffing out of me. You see a lot in twenty years at this work and especially since this war began, but something like this—no. I can't. Poor kids, so young. And I didn't dare look at them. That one over there, how old could he be? Eighteen at the most. And the one next to him? Maybe twenty. I was shaking from head to foot. And what if—what if my own son were there, with them, in a basket? No, no, think. You have a letter from him dated ten days ago; it takes more than that to amputate and for the wound to heal sufficiently to tolerate being transported.

The nurse's aides also drew back in horror. I took hold of myself in front of them. You're the head nurse, I told myself, you're in charge of this service. Straighten up. And I gave an order to the others: "Get acquainted with them between now and meal-time."

Each had his dog-tag around his neck. "How do you feel, Johann? Not too tired from the trip?" And so on from one basket to the next. Stupid words. What was there to say to them? They didn't need anything anymore. They were nothing but a digestive tract, dolls to be washed. No, they still had a brain and a heart, thought and speech, reason and consciousness. What was there to do? What was there to do for these poor kids? I was in despair. Talk to them? About their family, their home, their fiancées, their profession? They were all so weary, so sad. Their eyes seemed to say: What's the use?

Let's see, we could put on some music. The best would be a

movie—there was no television in those days. Read to them? Who'd do it? Just caring for their bodies took all our time, mine and my two helpers'.

When, kneeling beside the baskets, we had to unroll the bandages covering those human trunks to check on the scarring process, then wrap them up in fresh bandages, each of us wondered whether she could do it forty times a day. One of my aides said: "I'm going to use up here the whole supply of pity God gave me for a lifetime."

Kneeling down to wash them, kneeling for the basin, kneeling for the meals, in a day or two our backs were killing us. I like my patients to be clean, to look neat. We shaved them, though not all the same day, of course. We had to bring in pails of hot water from the kitchen, empty the dirty water in the gutter. The plumbers were taking their time. It meant added fatigue for us, but for them it helped while away the time, it was a distraction. And kneeling down beside the baskets to feed them, with one arm we'd prop up their busts—and how skimpy those busts were— there isn't any bulk to a man who has no arms, and his head seems huge—and we'd spoon-feed them. That also took time.

Some of them were upset about not getting mail. And yet they had a serial number and a postal code, like all other army men, and parents always write. I explained to them that, with their transfer, mail must have been delayed, that soon they'd be getting a whole pack of letters, all at once. "You'll hold them in front of me so I can read them myself, won't you, Mutti." After a few days I knew each one's first name. They called me Mutti, Mummy. I called them my darlings, my little ones.

During the six weeks they were with me, not a single letter arrived. One evening, as I was tucking him in one of the youngest said to me, "My parents live pretty near here. My mother would come to see me if she knew where I was."

"Very well, we'll write to her," I said. "Tell me her address. I'll mail the letter in town." Then I added: "You're not afraid it'll be hard on her? Don't you want to wait a little?"

"Wait for what? For my arms to grow back?"

I was ashamed of what I'd said. If he could bear it, wouldn't his mother be able to? "Write to her right away. I'd be so happy to see her! She's very pretty, my mom is, she's got long blond hair, soft, soft hair." I wrote, providing my own address for her answer. I don't know why, but I didn't quite trust the post office. In the evening—we alternated nights on duty, my assistants and I—I would go from one basket to the other. I'd give the boys a good-night kiss, stroke their brows: "Sleep tight, my dear, see you tomorrow." I'd switch off the big bulb, leaving the night light, and I'd look at those lined-up baskets in the dim blue light—men, lives. And settling myself in the nook I'd fixed up behind a curtain, I would weep. I would have preferred never to go home; I dreaded the moment when I had to leave the ward behind me. When I came in, from within the baskets eyes would turn in my direction, I'd smile with my heart in my mouth, feeling weak in the knees, feeling my hands shake. I'd try to pluck up courage for them: perhaps, I'd tell myself, perhaps they're here while waiting to be equipped. They make extraordinary artificial limbs nowadays, and, what with the war, this art is being perfected. However, regarding them the hospital director knew nothing. Amputees had been shipped to us, that was all.

You imagine you grow accustomed to anything. You can't get used to seeing men who've been cut in two. My nerves were giving out. And there was that vision that haunted my sleep insistently, that vision of my son, lying without arms or legs at the bottom of a laundry basket.

I had just obtained a radio for the ward when army trucks arrived at our door to pick up the baskets with my patients in them. They cried as they left: "Mutti, Mutti, what about the letters? You think they'll be sent on to us?" "Of course, my darlings, I'll see to it that they are," and I gave them a last kiss on the forehead, a last little touch of my lips on their eyelids.

That same day the Gestapo called me in. An officer asked me point blank: "Was it you who wrote this letter?" He handed me the one I'd written to the young boy's mother.

49

"Yes, I did."

"This is the Third Reich's business, you shouldn't interfere in it."

"I wasn't interfering in anything, I was just helping a poor kid who wanted to see his mother again."

"From now on you'll tend to your own business," and two policemen escorted me to Ravensbrück without my being authorized to make a stop at home or to inform anyone.

When the war ended and I returned to Vienna I went to my hospital and questioned my co-workers and the director. "What happened to my patients, the boys in the laundry baskets?" Nobody knew. The assumption was that they had been taken off to a gas chamber.

I did think of writing to the boy's mother. But I had forgotten her address. Then I decided not to write even if it came back to me. Better that they be left to believe their children had been killed at the front. It's hard enough as it is to lose a son. But I'll never forget those little ones of mine, those young fellows lined up in laundry baskets, under the bluish glow of the night light.

XII

—Had someone told us, when we were there, had we known that we would meet again, thirty-eight years later, on the California coast . . .

—To know we'd come back, that would have changed everything at the time, when death hovered over us, when we were at life's lowest ebb, with no hope left.

—There were some who never stopped believing they'd make it back . . .

—You really think there were any like that?

—Yes, there were some who without having the least certainty, and all the while knowing how hypothetical it was, there were some who never stopped believing they'd get back. The optimists. A very strengthening thing, optimism!

—Were you one of those? I wasn't. I wanted to believe I'd come back because to stop believing in it meant giving up. I forced myself to believe without ever convincing my rational self. I was desperate. It's strange, this desire to live. In my head, rationally, I knew it was impossible to make it through, but my body persisted in wanting to live. It was as though I was composed of two independent beings.

—I wouldn't say I was an optimist, but I fought with a kind of energy I didn't believe I was capable of. I fought. Period. Fortunately, we were given a breather in Raisco. Once out of Birkenau, we regained a reasonable hope, regained some strength too. If we hadn't been transferred from Birkenau to Raisco I wouldn't have recovered from typhus. The work there was less hard, there was water to drink.

—And we received packages. For us Frenchwomen, they were the first ones since we'd been away. At last people in our family knew where we were. But how few of us there were after six months in Birkenau. Well, let's not start in on the old memories. It's something I never do.

—Nor do I.

—Still, I would like to know . . . When we ran into each other in Paris—that was in the Fall of 1945, and you were getting ready to set out for the United States—you told me that you had escaped from Raisco. The people I was with had long since left there for Ravensbrück. It was so soon after the return and I was so mixed up that I can't recall what you told me. Perhaps you never did tell me about it. All that was the past and the thing I had to do was get back into the present. I had the feeling I was wandering in a fog. You, on the other hand, seemed so clear-minded.

—I don't know whether I was really all there. I did the things that had to be done, methodically, carefully, but as if I were two people in one. Nevertheless, I got everything done that had to be done.

—When exactly did you escape from Raisco?

—When the SS evacuated Auschwitz. They began by emptying Birkenau. The dying women were abandoned; all the prisoners in the smaller camps around about the big Auschwitz for-men-only camp were gathered together. And all of a sudden, on the morning of the 20th of January, the word came down for everybody to line up in front of the gate. I made up my mind in a flash. The Russians are coming. They'll be here tomorrow or the next day (I had heard this from Polish prisoners who were in touch with the partisans. You know that our partisans often came close to the camp and brought us news). And for two or three days we had been hearing explosions going on day and night: the gas chambers and the crematoriums were being blown up. The SS were obliterating all traces. They were going to transfer us to another camp, in Germany. Good. If I hide here, I said to myself, I'll see the Russians arrive. Being Polish, who knows whether they'll liberate me right away. Neither did I want to wait for the war to end in a camp in Germany. Auschwitz is in Poland, and Poland's pretty near liberated. So I hid in one of the greenhouses. When the camp had been cleared out and everyone was gone, I came out of my hiding place and started on my way.

There was snow on the ground, the temperature was twenty below. I headed in the direction of Warsaw. It was safe going provided I kept away from the German rear-guard and the advancing Russian lines. In the first farm I stopped at I found some partisans. I was much too exhausted to join them. All I recall is that I slept for two days and nights under a thick, flower-covered comforter, and that a woman made me drink hot milk. When I was able to leave, she gave me a skirt, a scarf and some boots—the boots were a little large for me; they belonged to her son, who was off in the forest (we say "in the forest," you call it the maquis) but I put a little straw in them and off I went.

I walked from one village to the next, went from one house to another. The countryside had not suffered too much from the war, the hamlets being scattered and far off the highways. People were poor but they always had their thick, hot soup, milk, and a corner where I could sleep. They would steer me onto the safest road. Sometimes a peasant would give me a lift in his cart. Ah, the horses were thin and tired. The best ones had been requisitioned by the occupying forces. Sometimes too I'd get a ride in the car of the former underground patrols, now operating in broad daylight. All those I met questioned me about Auschwitz, asking me whether I had come across this or that member of their family. And what about gas chambers? It was true, wasn't it? Finally, after three weeks of walking through snow-covered country, I saw Warsaw in the distance.

My city was unrecognizable: nothing but ruins and wreckage, and under the snow it more resembled some old engraving than what I remembered. People were living there, however, in cellars, in bits of still standing structures, in improvised shelters. Strangely, in this annihilated city, the lay-out of the streets was still there. It had an unreal look. I came upon former friends who at once offered to take me in. Once I was a little stronger, I began to hunt for my relatives, other friends. I went at it street by street, one neighborhood after the other, often till nightfall. At night, a kind of magic transformed the ruins. From their desolateness arose a phantasmagoria out of a dream: against the milky backdrop of the sky stood out the odd silhouettes of walls, piles of stone. I walked in a sort of dizzy elation, a ghost in a ghostly setting.

I found some of my friends. It was amazing: I had come out of Auschwitz, they had got through the bombings, the Gestapo, famine, the dreadful cold. The missing were more numerous than the survivors, however.

I found the people to whom my sister, a nurse, had entrusted her children before joining the underground. It was a couple of kilometers out of town. The children were in good health, but their eyes . . . their blue eyes seemed veiled by a film of gray. I took them in my arms; they kissed me, without their faces brightening, without any light coming into their eyes. I still see the three of them as I found them there, huddled together in front of the fire like so many frightened kittens. When shall I see them smile again? Their father, an officer in the underground army, had been caught and shot. Their mother—my sister—had been hanged. In your country, in France, the Nazis didn't hang women; they deported them. In our country they shot the men and hanged the women, sometimes from trees, and left the corpses hanging for a number of days. To put fear into the population. Before my arrest I knew I'd never see my sister again, nor her husband, and I knew that if I survived I'd take charge of her children, a girl and two boys. The people who had looked after them proved unbelievably generous. They had taken care of and now returned to me my sister's things, her fur coat and jewels and would not keep a penny of the money she had left to cover the children's expenses. I was able to recover some more money belonging to my parents—my parents, who had died before the war, had been wealthy. The war was over now and I made an immediate decision. After seeing the Russian army established in Warsaw, I realized Poland was never going to be free again. Our holdings in Lithuania had been annexed by the Soviets. What I now had to do was gather together everything I could take with me and then leave.

The administration was gradually reorganizing, life was resuming. I made preparations for my departure. That meant distributing bribes left and right—when I think about it! I handed out my mother's diamonds like small change. Anyhow, what are diamonds? Auschwitz had taught us to value things only for their usefulness. In exchange for a part of my fortune I obtained passports and exit visas. And that's how you saw me in Paris, with my niece and two nephews, in the fall of 1945.

—I remember the children—so very blond, so very well-behaved, also so sad.

—They remained sad and overly well-behaved for a long time.

I had left Warsaw not knowing the whereabouts of my fiancé, who had been in the underground too. Was he dead, alive, a prisoner? Staying in Poland waiting of news of him wouldn't have done any good. I made up my mind to wait in Paris while friends in the United States took the necessary steps to enable us to immigrate. And all of a sudden, in Paris, there was my fiancé! He had searched for me also, and found out from Warsaw friends that I had left. I had been careful to tell everyone I knew that I'd be staying at a hotel near the Etoile, where I'd been with my father before the war. The hotel still existed, still had the same name. For me, Paris had hardly changed. I showed it to the children in the long walks I took with them, revisiting the haunts of my adolescence: the Tuileries, the quays along the Seine. How beautiful Paris was, and how happy to have become herself again, despite the heavy restrictions still in force.

Joe did not have the difficulty I had in getting out of Poland. Dressed in his captain's uniform, with papers ordering him abroad—on a mission he'd devised for himself: no more underground, he and his friends were the general staff now—he had traveled across Germany without a hitch. He thought, as I did, that the best solution was to emigrate to the United States. He was unwilling to accept Soviet domination. Bear in mind that he had seen his regiment crushed by the Red Army in '39, that he had escaped by a miracle and had immediately formed a group of partisans, the beginning of the underground army which plagued the Nazis and which did not always receive help from the Russians. Emigrate. Perhaps for you that's the formerly wealthy bourgeois' reaction in the face of Communism. No. It was the feeling every Pole had, I assure you. The Russians had oppressed us for too long, betrayed us on every occasion. Joe and I had the means to leave, that was the only difference. Hitler had been toppled, but Poland was still vanquished.

I left Warsaw which was slowly rising from its ruins. People had only the most miserable of tools. Mostly they used their bare hands. I had fought with my people, now I was abandoning it. But I feared a repression which was rearing its ugly head. To go from Auschwitz to a Siberian camp, never! And the children? I'll never see my country again. For the children, a new life is starting. For you, life is starting again.

My fiancé and I were married in New York. After first getting his bearings, my husband chose to go to the West Coast. Ever since the war California had been booming. It wasn't a bad idea, as you can see. My husband has done pretty well. We've had three childen of our own. Yes, I'm the mother of a family of six. Every one has gone to college. My nephews are married; our own children will soon be off on their own too.

—What happened to your illusions—sorry, maybe I should say your fond feelings about the United States when the Vietnam War came along?

—I never harbored any illusions as regards the United States. Joe and I simply felt that Europe would not offer us the same possibilities for raising our children, for starting a new life. When we became involved in the war in Vietnam, we had only one concern: that our sons not go. Had they been drafted, we'd have got them to desert. Canada, Sweden offered asylum to draft resisters, and we had the means to provide for them there. Oh no, those children are not going to fight in any war. Luckily, my nephews were in college and getting good grades, so they were deferred. Our own son was too young and the war ended before he was old enough to be called. I can tell what you are about to say: that this is an individual solution. Sure it is. Is there any other course? I joined every protest movement, went on marches, took part in every demonstration, signed every petition— unhappily, without much confidence in their effectiveness.

—How strange it feels listening to your story with the Pacific Ocean out there. Whenever I think of you, I see you in your striped dress, a scarf on your head, I see your chalky pallor, I hear your hoarse voice. Sitting here, I ask myself whether I'm dreaming, or whether what I hear is your from-beyond-Auschwitz voice.

XIII

WARSAW

i

Night shapes
livid faces
they issue from darkness
hollowed pupils in eyes of stone
they exchange glances eyelids lowered
weapons pass from sleeve to sleeve
weapons patiently amassed
at the price of what hungers
of what perils.
They issue from shadow
quickly sink back again
weapons emerge from every nook
from every cranny
every alleyway
glide shadows
night shadows slip through the night.
Each furtive shape knows where to go
what to do
where to set the firebrands
and scrawny urchins let go their mothers' bloodless hands
to run to where the fighters are
also to do
what they have to do.

Without any signal suddenly
the shooting starts
flames rise to the sky
together with the prayers of the elders

they who say one must be reasonable.
Rebellion stirs the ghetto
spurs men ready to die
but as an act of will
not herded to the abattoir.
When the enemy machineguns are set in place
the streets empty in a flash
the enemy shoots blindly
and from places invisible
other firing replies
from rooftops, cornices,
ground-level vents
and everything obstructs its advance
baby carriages, ladders, scaffolding
old tools
the ancient rubbish from cellars
bric-à-brac from attics
the ghetto throws everything into battle
turns all its own into weapons.

They were not willing to die in Auschwitz
heaven heard them
they made an attempt
the elders were right
but it's they who will be leaving tomorrow
for the gas chambers
along with the women and the babes
who had remained hidden in the lofts.
The fighters once again become shadows
that dawn etches on the pavement.

ii

By the cannonade moving closer
clearer
ever clearer amidst the rustle of leaves

the sky filling with different airplanes
they know the time has come
to leave the forests.
For five years concealed
in the tunnels they dug
their weapons at hand
they lay burrowed.
They come out to set ambushes
a staff car blows up and burns
a trapped tank sinks in a tangle of branches
they come out to capture a supplies convoy
to get hold of food and ammunition
they come out to derail trains
loaded with enemy troops
crossing their country toward the front
further east
they are men for every form of combat
all-purpose men
apt at everything
elusive
quick and lean like wolves in winter.
The attack concluded
they sink into the forest
re-enter their holes
count heads
Alas
but yesterday's small boys grown now
almost into men
take to the forest in their turn
and fill the gaps.

The hour has come
they feel it
it's time to leave the shadows
there are signs everywhere in the forest
they've learned to decipher the signs

they've also learned
for they have friends posted everywhere
that the enemy is falling back
that it's retreating towards the capital
all its forces are converging there
and digging in for a rear-guard battle
the last one before Berlin.
They know the eastern allies are approaching
so
head in their direction
open the way for them
so they who know every pathway
they leave the forest
in small groups they infiltrate their city
set up command posts
their communications network
they know just how to do it
having spent years organizing
in the depths of the forest
having learned years ago
to do everything
with nothing at all.
To lie in hiding no longer
to fight at last in broad daylight.
There's joy in their eyes
confidence in their manner and grace
and in the reclaimed town
every passer-by is their brother
every girl their fiancée
the crowd their accomplice
sharing a common language.
A splendid summer

And when the allies appear
on the opposite bank of the river
halting there

surely gathering themselves to spring
they unleash the attack within the city
from everywhere at once.
Sudden fires glow in the lavender summer sky.
Come on in
everything's waiting for you
it's spelled out for anyone with eyes to see
what's written in the dancing flames
it roars forth in explosions and firing.

Deaf blind
the allied army does not budge
it bivouacs on the river's edge
waiting for what?
Are not its soldiers in need of rest
who've marched from the Volga
at last a river to bathe in
mild summer nights at last.
The allied army does not budge.
It will allow the partisans
to be killed to the last man
and will advance into the city's smoking ruins
when the unequal fight has ended
when hope's army
has been crushed.
Then it will enter the city
the mute city
dead Warsaw
humbled, betrayed
Warsaw a dagger in the heart.

iii

They've drawn shut the arsenal gates
closed the grates at the pitheads
locked the gates of factories

behind the gates and grates
they're at home
with one another
free behind the gates
joyous
free to ask questions
Why? why?
Every man needs to know why
every man has the right to know why
They have asked questions already
shots fired by the militia were the answer
they went back to work
without having answers
they buried their dead
without knowing what to tell them.

Again they asked the questions
in nineteen seventy-six
they held for a long time behind their gates
no answer came
the tanks broke through the gates
they buried their dead
rage in their hearts.

This time
they must be answered
Why work six days a week
to earn less than enough to live
why dig coal out of the ground
without having anything to heat with
why
when the soil produces
have not enough to eat
why constant scarcity
poverty
the war ended long ago

why then
has no one the right
to ask questions.
Silence! Get down to work! And hang your head!
Bend the knee? No.
This time it's enough
enough toiling without hope in sight
enough toiling without knowing why.
Every man has the right to speak out
They've posted comrades
to guard the gates
behind the gates
they're home
they can speak
talk
question those who know
understand why nothing works
learn where the fruits of their labor go.
We're the many
let's not forget our strength!
And throughout the country
behind factory gates
deep inside mines
by the forges at the arsenals
there's a flood of questions.
Every man has the right to know
the why of his work
of his life
of his hardships
Surely there is an explanation.

The men in power will brook no questions
They think in terms of numbers.
Underlying the numbers are workers
about whom the government does not want to be bothered
the workers are to work

they exist for that only
Who's egging them to ask questions?
Malignant subversion
leading them astray
We'll bring them to their senses.

Behind the gates
before the halted machines
the workers have forged their tools
the tools of revolt
they have found answers to the questions
they have found solutions.
Let's take our affairs in hand
and make things work.

The country is bankrupt
its remedy
to declare war upon the working men.
Leaders, just think a little
without them you are nothing
without them you can do nothing.
Think? You consult your breviary
the breviary of the neighbor who watched
Warsaw bleed to death
in order to enter as the victor there
and to impose his rule.
Off to prison with the workers
the teachers and all who think.

Eyes are veiled
lips tight
wordless is the mouth
stony the gaze
night falls over Warsaw.

XIV

If I ever return . . . that's how our wildest dreams began back there.

If I ever get back, I'll go to Greece. I made myself this promise as though it were the simplest thing in the world. Viewed from Auschwitz, everything was simple and fabulous. Going to Greece was as fabulous as going to the moon. And just as simple: all that was required was to return home. Once there, everything would be easy. Everything would be possible. How many plans were dashed to pieces upon the reefs of reality, upon returning. Upon returning, life was difficult. Difficult to get accustomed to again, difficult to find one's way in. The most difficult was to recapture the desire to carry out the dreams that had helped one to survive back there. The impossible things we had dreamt of, now possible, no longer awakened our desire. We were too tired. Those things from which we had expected such delight—eating, taking a bath, strolling in a park—now cost us inordinate effort. The least decision exhausted us. How to start . . . Not to mention money, which was never considered back there when we would dream of doing this or that. Had we so lost all recollection of financial concerns, had we forgotten that trips are expensive? In dreams there are no obstacles. And so back there we had really dreamt.

This time, however, it was true. The incredible had occurred. I'd come out of the camp alive and now I was in Greece. Everything confirmed it: the light-colored short-sleeved dress I was wearing, the pink laurel bushes, the odors, the colors, the sky. Greece was the way I had wanted it. Everything delighted me. After two years spent in a kind of fog where nothing reached my conscious mind, I had regained my strength and vitality. I wanted to look at everything, to absorb beauty, to savor every instant, every mouthful of life.

Traces of the war had not yet disappeared. Roads were pitted, facades were scarred from the fighting. In 1948 the civil war which had followed the war against Hitler was drawing to a close. Markos, the guerilla leader, had vanished, the partisan forces, dissolved, were being rounded up. But that wasn't the Greece I had come to see. I was here for Delphi, Olympia, all the magical names from my schoolbooks. Political goings-on, recent events didn't interest me. I didn't wish to be distracted from my dream come true.

Seated outside a little café, I was gazing at the Parthenon, golden in the light of the setting sun, when a man at a nearby table, eyeing the number tattooed on my left forearm, addressed me: "An Auschwitz number, isn't it? I know what it is. At the main bookstore in Salonika there's a woman who's got one. She works in the French books section."

"So there's a Jewish woman from Salonika who survived? I thought not one was left."

"Oh yes, I believe a few survived."

The shipment of Salonika Jews arrived in Auschwitz two and a half months after our convoy got there, in April 1943. At Birkenau all we saw were women; the men were put in the Auschwitz camp for men. Some of those women spoke French, most spoke a Spanish from the time of Cervantes, even more ancient, dating from the period when Jews had been obliged to convert to Catholicism or leave Spain. They had resettled everywhere around the Mediterranean. In Salonika they made up a particularly flourishing community and that entire community had been transported to Auschwitz. Those Greek women perished rapidly. Probably because they were used to a sunny climate, to fresh fruit, they were more vulnerable than others to vitamin deficiency; it took only a few days and they were dead of scurvy and diarrhea.

Naturally, as soon as they entered the camp we went up to them to get news, to find out where the front was, how the war was going. They didn't know much. They may perhaps have known but they were so stunned after the trip and the shock of arrival that they were in a virtual stupor.

One of the first I spoke with was a rather heavy woman dressed in the uniform of a Soviet paratrooper. The Germans had apparently seized a quantity of these uniforms on the Russian front and had sent them to the camp for Jewish women to wear, Jewish women not being entitled to the striped dress. The poor soul had on a pair of pants like a motorcyclist's, much too tight at the waist so that the fly remained wide open. Grotesque, pitiful. Of course it wouldn't be long before those pants were too big . . .

"When I think that in Salonika I had two maids to look after me and now I haven't a bit of string to fasten my galoshes."

The snow had given way to deep, glue-like mud in which our galoshes would get stuck. They came loose all the time, and you had to stop constantly, bend down and use both hands to pull them from the mud, meanwhile receiving blows on the back because you had to keep moving. The mud season was the worst of all.

This woman spoke an almost literary French, addressing me with the formal *vous*. "We've been misled, shamefully misled. We were informed by the rabbis, who told us to get ready to leave for a city in which all the Jews of Europe were being regrouped, and that we were to take along everything that would be of use in our new home, everything except furniture. We packed dishes, bed and table linen, towels, blankets. If I hadn't been told this by people I trusted, you can be sure I'd have put my jewelry away in safekeeping. Instead, I took everything: money, silverware, family treasures above all. If the rabbis had not misled us—they themselves were probably misled, but how is it they suspected nothing at all?—some of us would have gone into hiding, got away. I prevented my son from doing so. I'll never forgive myself. Eighteen years old. And where is he now? All of us. All of us. They got every one of us."

"Never mind the jewelry and the silverware! Now what you have to do is think about saving your life."

"I'll never see Salonika again."

"Everyone feels that way when he first gets here. Even so, you've got to fight. You've got to fight."

"When we found ourselves in those cattle-cars, then we knew we had to expect the worst. But a horror like . . ."

She was standing in the mud, defenseless, dazed.

"If only I could find a bit of string."

Many of the Greek women were used for experiments. To study fertility, or sterility, we heard. Some who survived those operations were brought back to Birkenau where they died in short order. One day I was told by my friend Carmen that a Greek woman had just come up from the hospital. "She found no one left from her group. She showed me her belly. What a sight! Sewn up in every direction. An American patchwork quilt. You must go speak to her. She's all alone in the midst of the Polish women."

We went to see her that evening after roll-call. We talked for a little while. "See you tomorrow," we said when we left her. The next day she was nowhere to be found.

And one of those women had returned. I was tempted to take the train to Salonika. One likes to find out how stories end. My courage deserted me. Auschwitz will pursue me forever, it has pursued me even here. Will I ever escape it?

Tomorrow I'll go to Epidaurus.

XV

The column came into sight at the far end of the esplanade and advanced toward the dock. It must have come from the railroad station, a little station so nearly deserted that one could assume it was out of service. A while back, however, a train had been heard, the sound of a little steam engine of the sort you used to see on the secondary lines. As the column drew nearer you could distinguish men with something still of the look of soldiers. Miserable soldiers, trudging along, roughly four abreast at the head of the column, in disorder at the rear. All in the remnants of uniforms or rather in the semblance of uniforms made up of odds and ends which were nothing but rags and tatters.

The column advanced slowly. The men were trudging painfully because of their dilapidated shoes, because of the fatigue that showed in their drooping shoulders, their heavy heads, their faces half-hidden by beard, by rags tied round their necks and by their various head-coverings: berets, forage-caps, knitted woollen hats surmounted by pompons, bits of cloth rolled into turbans. As for the officers on either side of the column, they were nattily outfitted, as officers of victorious armies always are; each carried a revolver in a shining leather holster, his hands free.

The men trudged forward. Each had a tightly-rolled blanket slung bandoleer-wise over one shoulder, a haversack on the other. Almost all had a bundle of belongings in one hand. A small bundle. A defeated soldier doesn't have much left. Some had a tin mug hanging from a rope, a belt thanks to which the whole sad business was held together.

They drew near. No, these weren't soldiers, they were prisoners. They had the typical prisoner's dirty-looking stubble. You could barely make out their eyes, with those beards and the tangles of dark hair falling over their foreheads. Young men.

They headed toward the pier where a large caïque was tied up.

The officers waved the few passers-by out of the way. The prisoners advanced with blank faces. The passers-by withdrew. I just stood there, pretending not to understand the officers' signs. A woman standing near me, no doubt in reply to my questioning look, murmured something in Greek of which all I could make out was the word Makronisos, then she moved off. The men were People's Army guerillas who were being deported to the island of Makronisos, turned into a concentration camp.

In this month of May 1948, the partisans were in daily retreat, and the Royal Hellenic Army was winning back the ground they had occupied, nearly the whole of Greece at one point, from the Peloponnesus to Macedonia. The Royal Army still had to reconquer the mountains of the north and the northeast, on the Bulgarian border, and then the war would be over. For how long, for how many years would these men I was looking at remain on Makronisos? Weariness painted resignation on their faces. From what jails had they been extracted and for how many weeks, how many months had they been packed in them, beaten, interrogated? During what interminable transits had they waited, lying on the ground, without washing or shaving, before being transferred to Nauplia where they would board the boat for Makronisos?

I looked at the advancing men, I looked at them, I looked at them. I looked at them in order to meet their eyes, to meet the glance of some one of them who would be able to tell from mine that I knew.

It didn't happen. Dazed by fatigue, the men shuffled blindly forward. Despite the officer, who however did not dare shove me aside, I remained there, seeking that glance, a glance to which mine would have said "Courage, old brother! You'll make it back. I know that one can make it back. Don't let go." What could I do to convey my warm feelings to these men? To convey the intensity of the determination I wanted to instill in their veins, that determination to make it come hell or high water and to come out alive, the determination that had sustained me? Nothing. There wasn't anything I could do. Nothing that could help them. I didn't even have a clean handkerchief on me. I'd set out from Nauplia early in the morning to visit Epidaurus and nothing remained of the sandwiches I had taken with me to eat sitting on the theater's stone tiers, amidst the smell of the pines and the pink laurel in flower. What a lovely May day it had been, as I took in the full sweep of the vast theater. And now these men. Keeping my eyes on them, I rummaged angrily through my handbag. I did manage to come up with an already opened pack of cigarettes. I gave it a toss. One of them caught it in midair with the quick, nimble movement of someone who knows how not to attract attention. A veteran prisoner, that one. And had he noticed with what speed I'd calculated my throw so as to get the pack to him between two of the officers, just as they had their backs turned? Had he recognized me? Recognized the former prisoner in me? He had stuffed the pack into a pocket of his jacket and kept on walking. He hadn't even glanced at me.

The column halted at the gangplank, a crude bit of plank. The men set their bundles down, waited, then, one by one, they began to go aboard by way of that shaky piece of wood.

Evening fell over the bay, the sea turned dark blue, and the sky darkened while remaining blue, the lilac blue of fading lavender. On its islet a stone's throw from the mainland, the little fortress of Bourzi, once a prison, switched on its lights.

There I stood, stood stupidly, like the passers-by who had paused to watch us leave from Compiègne on that Sunday, January 24, 1943, and had then turned their heads away.

I lingered for a long time on the deserted quay but had to leave before the boat set sail. I was trembling from helplessness as one trembles from the cold.

Since then I have often gone back to Greece.

Today, in Nauplia, the sailboats, the beach . . .

XVI

She is sitting in the shade of the white wall
in front of her house
with others
also old women
yet not so old as she
shrivelled
bent over withered
her face all creased
a web of wrinkles surrounding her faded eyes.
The others knit or embroider
she
does nothing
she's there
emptied of life
her eyes discolored from weeping
hands knotted from having prayed
lips pursed to nothingness
from having ceased to speak.

Her eyes see nothing save that day
her memory has retained that day alone
on that day her life became suspended
the day her three sons
along with all the young men of the village
were taken away
locked up by the *Kommandantur*
to be shot
with all the boys from the village
the boys between sixteen and twenty
that day
her three sons.

The priest undertook to sway the major
tried to change his mind
These poor parents
are you going to take their three children from them
their three sons
that's all they have in the world
must they be left with nothing?

I am willing to spare one
said the major
let them chose which of the three.

The priest related this to the father and the mother
the father has died since then
the mother
she's the old woman with faded eyes.
Choose
choose
can one choose amongst one's children
the one who'll remain alive?
Torn apart
smitten down
what must they do?
Choose.
They were not able to.
The old Cretan looks at me with her fixed look
and says:
Pray God never to send you
all that a woman's heart can bear.

That day
it was a summer's day
when Hitler was conquering the world.

All that
the heart of a woman can bear.

THE MADWOMEN OF MAY

Round and round they go
mad women
round the plaza they go
the madwomen of May
round the Plaza de Mayo
round they go
mad from worry
mad from anxiety
mad from pain
round and round the Plaza de Mayo
go the madwomen of May.

So anguish-stricken they cannot cry out
cannot cry out
for the knot in their throat
for the pain
which grips their whole body
so strong
they cannot cry forth
for the dry terror in their heart.

At twilight
they arrive
by all the streets leading into the plaza
arrive at the rendezvous
rendezvous of unbearable distress
arrive to cry out in silence
since their throats can no longer shout.
They greet each other with glances
at one another smile

thin smiles.
A newcomer.
Who are you? From where?
My husband
last night
all morning I've run everywhere
everywhere wooden doors
iron faces
we don't know anything
come back tomorrow
wooden doors leaden silence.

Another new face. Who are you? Where are you from?
My son
a student
last night
this very night.

At each foregathering their number grows
and on the square the circling ring widens.

Round and round they go the madwomen of May
Round and round and their whole being shrieks
their tight-locked mouths shriek
a shriek that won't come forth
a blank shout
their bodies torn and their tears run dry
useless nails
dug into hardened palms.

Round they go gone mad from anxiety
round they go gone mad from pain
and that shriek you do not hear
echoes throughout the whole world.
It rings in faraway ears
their cry

but beating upon the walls of the May Palace
upon the walls round the Plaza de Mayo
it draws no echo.
Unresponding the walls are deaf
deafer still the torturers
faceless the butchers.
Where is my husband, cries this one here
Where is my husband
cry a thousand others.
You tortured him
in your cellars in your barracks
in your torture chambers
you tortured him and with him then did what?
What did you do with him after
After?
Give us at least his torn body
give us his broken limbs
give us his crushed hands
give them back to us
so that we may know
give them back to us
so that we may bury them.

Where is my son shriek a thousand others
Where are all my sons shrieks yet another
Say what you did with them
Say it say
what did they do to you
those innocent souls?
Give us his face trampled beneath your boots
give us his eyes you made squirt from their sockets
give us his burst open head
and that brown curl he'd twist round his finger
while he was reading
give them back to us
give them back to us

that we may know
give them back to us
that we may bury them.

Desaparecidos
What do you mean disappeared?
A man doesn't disappear
who knows his way home
a man doesn't disappear
who knows his wife
is waiting for him at home.
A boy his mother has sent to the store
doesn't disappear
thousands of men don't disappear
without their footsteps leaving any trace
the weight of a man's step
leaves its mark on the road
so does the weight of a man's life.
Disappeared
how dare you.

Mine left for work
in the morning as usual
no one saw him there
he didn't return.

Mine left for court
no one heard him there
he did not come back
the man he was to defend disappeared too.

It was mine he was defending
a worker with broad hands
hands that earned the children's bread.

What was he guilty of

this one
what was he guilty of
that other?
Of having uttered words which displeased
perhaps
it's conjecture
one doesn't know what he was charged with
all died without having been charged
the accused and the lawyer
who was to have pleaded for him.

All died from having been tortured
for they're dead aren't they
at least say so.
In what mass graves
in what catacombs
in what charnel houses do you cast
all these men you murder
in what seas do you have them borne away
these men you torture to death
once dead
you've surely got to get rid of them
so where
where are they
where where where
tell us where they are.

Round and round they go
the madwomen of May
mad from pain
mad from woe

I hurt from his hands you crushed under your iron heels
his hands
and their caress alive upon my face
I hurt from his temples crushed by you

his temple close to mine in the warmth of the night
I hurt from his chest you crushed
burst lungs drowned heart
his chest which breathed against mine
when he'd greet me coming home in the evening.
I hurt in all his body you have snatched from me
bloodthirsty beasts
have you neither wife nor child
nor lover
inhuman brutes
have you never placed your cheek against a child's cheek
your hand in a woman's hand
given your eyes to the eyes of another who loves you
brutes
what then are you made of
brutes
not of the same flesh as we
human beings
how can you feign our appearance
when all of you disclaims
inclusion in our species.

Round and round they go
the madwomen of May
upon the Plaza de Mayo
go round in June and September
in winter and summer
they circle and they cry
cry their anger
mad from anxiety
mad from pain
mad from woe.

Tell us
what have you done
with our men with our children

what did you do with my husband
the lawyer
you smashed his throat to silence his voice
what did you do with my husband
the baker
the sweet aroma of bread in his hair
when he came up from kneading downstairs
the sweet aroma of bread
on his hands softened by flour
what did you do with my husband
the journalist
who knew lots of things and made them known
what did you do with my husband
the taxi driver
who knew all the ways and byways
you use to make men and their children disappear
what did you do with my husband
the doctor
his reassuring voice his look that helped to heal.
What did you do with my betrothed
so timid
he'd wait till nightfall to say he loved me.

Speak tell
into what ossuaries
into what graveyards
into what holes you threw
wrecked flesh slimy from suffering
skeletons stripped bare by your lashes
by your pincers
speak tell
what have you done with them?

Round and round they go
the madwomen of May
there are failed attempts

to silence them
the whole world hears their cry
the whole world hears and is still
indifferent
powerless
harassed in its own life
caring pitying helpless
is there truly nothing to be done?

Go round madwomen of May
go round till all the women of the world
make the rounds
before the palaces that rule us
pick up your cries
till those cries pierce the hearts
of those who traffic
with your torturers

Go round madwomen of May
round and round on the Plaza de Mayo
cry women of Buenos Aires
cry till the ghosts of your tortured rise
like so many staring eyes
staring into ours and accusing us
incandescent stares that burn
burning the skin from our souls
and causing us to scream from your pain
cry until the world
bursts from shame
go round
go round the Plaza de Mayo
madwomen of May

KALAVRITA OF THE THOUSAND ANTIGONES

Right here. Here it is. This is the path they took.

This isn't the earth they trod. These aren't the stones that rolled loose under their feet. This isn't the dry bed of the stream. That was their real path. The real path is underneath the steps, these steps of gold-colored stone cemented down over the real path to preserve its course, to prevent wear to the real path.

The steps of gold-colored stone lead up to the monument. There, up there on the hill.

The real path led them to their death, there, in that ravine on the side of the hill.

Let's go up. Below us we'll see the town and the school where the women with the children and the old people were locked in. See it? A little distance off from the houses.

The women were shut up inside the school, with the children and the old people.

The men were going up the path, this path now made of steps made out of gold-colored stone.

The women didn't know what was being done with the men. They didn't know and they were frightened. Some were screaming, and the others couldn't prevent them from screaming.

The men were climbing the hill. They walked in silence. Soldiers shouted to them to speed it up.

They took a long time to get up the hill. For the women who were locked inside the school, who were hugging their little ones to their bosoms, it seemed they were taking a long time to get up the hill.

For the men who were climbing, the path was short. They knew, the men did, that at the end of the path lay death. The way from here to death is always short. And even if the climb was hard, the time was short to them.

Stones rolled under the men's footsteps. Actually, it wasn't a path, I mean a regular path of the sort you take to go from here to there. It was a dry and stony furrow like the bed of a stream that stopped flowing long ago.

For the women, the path was interminable.

For the men, it was a shortcut.

A shortcut from life to death for those men whose life had not been fulfilled.

A shortcut from life to death for the boys not yet fully grown.

A shortcut from life to death for the older ones who wouldn't have their final illness, the one that puts you to bed, the one you die from.

The women, locked up with the children and the old people, under the guard of helmeted and armed soldiers, did not know where the men were, and what was being done with them. They feared the worst, but there are so many times when you feared the worst and it didn't happen . . .

Those who weren't screaming begged the screaming ones to keep still, to keep still so they could hear noises and from those noises know what was happening. Then there was stillness and they all listened and nothing in the silence told what was happening on the hill. There was only a dog barking.

All of them wondered what they had done with the men after having pushed them into a corner of the square while they, with the little ones and the old people, were pushed into the school.

The men who were climbing the path didn't know what had become of the women and children while they were climbing to their appointment with death, and the thought of their wives and children made the blood pound in their hearts.

They were going to their appointment with death, but it was not a true appointment since their lives were still incomplete, since it isn't natural that all the lives of the men living in a particular place end on the same day, at the same spot.

It was a false appointment, wasn't it, since no one had seen the sign death always makes to you when the hour is at hand. Death was there without anyone having seen it come, without anyone having heard its call, without anyone having felt its touch in a dream the night before.

One mustn't trust the things you're told. In those years, all appointments with death were true.

Inside the school, the women began to scream again, hugging their terrified children tighter to their bosoms, children so terrified the poor things didn't make a sound, their lips white and their eyes wide open and staring. And the women were all thinking so hard about the men that they didn't stop to comfort the old people, ready to collapse but trying to appear calm. For them, it was their sons who were climbing up the hill. Their sons and grandsons. They didn't know this, but they were full of dread.

Perhaps the men who were climbing the hill heard the screams of the women. Afterwards all the women tried to believe they hadn't. No, I don't think the men heard. No, they mustn't have heard. Their ears were full of the buzzing which is the voice of death when it draws near.

Because while they were walking up the hill, they, the men, knew.

How can you not know, when death is ringing in your ears, when you are walking in a column and the column is flanked by machineguns, by soldiers carrying machineguns, soldiers in helmets and boots, the kind we lay in wait for in the mountains and ambushed precisely because they were the bearers of death?

No more ambushes now. All the men from the town were there, together with those from neighboring villages who had come to market that day. All the men were there because in winter you don't go to the fields.

The forces were more unequal than ever. All our men were caught.

The men were climbing the hill without saying anything. Why and to whom would they have said anything? All were to die at the same appointment. An appointment where words were wasted. Why speak to death? Nothing ever comes from its lips. And the words you want to say at that moment are for those who will go on, who will go on living and who will transmit to others what you said.

As for us, we know what they would have told us and we have done it.

We have brought up the children. We have looked after the animals and the trees. We have kept the soil under cultivation. We have kept the house. We have kept the memory.

The women were wondering what would happen to the men and all keenly regretted not having been able to offer them the least thing for the journey

a crust of bread and handful of olives for the road, for example

for they tried to tell themselves they'd collected them in order to take them far away. It had happened before; there were villages where all the men had been deported.

Each woman reproached herself for not having given her man a tender kiss when they woke that morning. One ought to have had some inkling and, once again, there had been no sign. It was a morning like any other morning.

A Saturday. Market-day. The market was on the square. Just where it continues to be held today. There wasn't much to buy at the market during those years, but the peasants from all around would come anyway. They brought the little they had, some onions, cheese, a tool to be mended by one of the town craftsmen. It was mainly to talk, to get news, that they came. And we, the town folk, though we knew there wasn't much to buy, we would come too. Out of habit, to talk, to hear news, to see people.

So, when the town was surrounded

in no time at all, suddenly all the streets leading to the marketplace were blocked;

when they had the town surrounded everyone was there on the public square, except the very old and women with nurslings, but the soldiers went from house to house breaking down the doors and with the butts of their rifles drove them out too

until everybody was on the square, like fish all caught in a net.

The circle tightened then, and the soldiers, with their boots and helmets, and their weapons at the ready, pushed the men over to one side,

the women and small children to the other,

following the orders that the officers, carrying only a pistol, were yelling in their language we didn't understand.

We were shoved from where we were at one edge of the square over to the other, with some substituting here and there.

This boy is at least sixteen, so into the men's group.

This old man must be over seventy, so over here, into the women's group.

The soldiers sorted everybody out, dragged this person from one group, drove him into another. To this side, the men from sixteen to seventy, to that side, the women along with the youngsters and the very old.

And while this sorting was going on, other soldiers ransacked the houses, dragging out those who were still hiding, the women who had recently given birth with their newborn in their arms, infirm grandmothers huddling in a dark corner of the fireplace. It was winter.

The soldiers dragged the priest out of the church and,

from his home

the finest house on the square,

the mayor who was putting on his Sunday best because he wanted to discuss matters with the officer. The officer shut him up with a blow of his fist and pushed him into the group of men. The priest wanted to lead everyone in a prayer. The officer shut him up too, and the priest also was pushed into the group of men.

The soldiers went about their work rapidly, methodically. You saw they were trained, used to doing this. In no time they had everything arranged. The men standing in ranks, the women over against the wall of the school,

squeezed tight together, and craning their necks to catch the eye of a husband, a son, a father.

Five of mine were in the column: my husband, my father, my two boys, and my father-in-law, who lived with us. My boys were seventeen, nineteen.

The column of men set off, with the soldiers escorting it. Meanwhile some other soldiers shoved us into the school, locked the doors and they all left except for four or five who were posted as guards. They needed soldiers on the hill. There were none too many for all that there was to do.

Thirteen hundred men. Thirteen hundred and two at the outset.

Brave, all of them, and who would have sold their lives dearly, but now without defense amidst those armed soldiers in boots and helmets. Defenseless, the innocent creatures. Slaughtered like pascal lambs.

The men were neither chained nor fettered. Chain all those men up? Imagine, the soldiers had no time to waste. They had other jobs to do, elsewhere. There were other villages on their way.

The soldiers had the men climb the hill, gun barrels shoved in their ribs.

Since the men were not tied, two managed to get away. They slipped out of the column. They crept into a gully, and from there they watched. It was from them we found out how everything happened. They told us how those walking right behind had moved up to fill the gap, edging them out on that side of the column where there was an interval between guards. What extra danger did those two run? They slipped out alive from among the dead.

Only two.

The men climbed the slope. It was pretty steep, as you can see for yourself. They reached the ravine. Over there, on your right. Here where we're standing we're already some distance out of town. They couldn't have heard the women shrieking inside the school building.

The soldiers had a hundred men at a time go down into the ravine where other soldiers had already taken up position, one knee on the ground, behind their machine guns. And in batches of a hundred the men were cut down.

From inside the school house we heard the machine guns and those who had been shrieking became still. The weight of the silence was unbearably heavy.

We strained our ears, listening to each outburst of firing, praying each time it was the last, and with our hands we covered the ears of the children who were hiding their faces in our bosoms. The machine guns fired on and off for three whole hours.

In three hours' time it was over.

When the entire column of our men had descended from the path into the ravine, where they now lay fallen in a heap, the soldiers dismounted their guns and the officer walked in his boots over the corpses, giving the coup de grace to anything still stirring. Then he put his pistol back into its holster, had his soldiers line up four abreast, and marched them back to the trucks they had parked on the edge of town.

The two who had hidden in the bushes described it all.

From inside the school, we heard the soldiers passing, the rhythmic pounding of boots.

Someone, in the school, said that now they would set fire to the building, that that had been done in other places, and some women began to scream again.

But no. Once the column of soldiers had marched past, another officer arrived, he unlocked the doors, and he left together with the four or five men who had stood guard outside the school.

Even with the doors open, we didn't dare move, we didn't dare step out.

We stayed there, motionless, hushing those who were screaming still, trying to figure out, as we listened to the silence, what we ought to do.

We waited, petrified with fear. The roar of the departing trucks had subsided when one of the two men who had escaped the massacre left his hiding place and came running to tell us that it was all over,

that they had all left, and that we could come out.

The other survivor had also left his hiding place under the brambles and, by way of the paths following the mountain ridges, he had run ahead to warn the other villages of the barbarians' coming. Since the trucks were traveling along the twisting road—a road where the turns are so sharp a driver has to do some backing up to get around them—the short cuts on the ridges got him there first,

and the men from the villages escaped into the mountains.

We walked out of the school house. We sent the old people home, leaving the littlest ones in their care, and we women, with the other children, the fourteen- and fifteen-year-olds, we went up to the ravine.

We held our hearts in both hands for what was to come.

Such was the beating of our hearts we thought they would burst from our bodies.

With both hands clamped above our breasts we strove to keep our racing hearts from bursting.

Our hearts beat so that we gasped for breath,

and yet our legs brought us to the edge of the ravine.

We had climbed the steep path where the footsteps of the men had left no mark. It was just what it is like after the passage of a flock. Dust and stones have no memory.

And our eyes,

while we were climbing the hill, holding our hearts in our two hands,

our eyes kept on searching the ground for some trace, some object that might have fallen from a pocket, something we would recognize.

We had climbed the hill, hands pressed to our hearts,

impatient to know,

while dreading to see what we we were about to see,

dreading it so that today we no longer know how we climbed that hill, how we had the strength to do it.

At the top of the path, here from where you can peer down into the ravine, at the top of the path the first ones saw

and they understood it was useless to hold their hearts in both hands: if they did not burst at once then they'd last a lifetime in spite of everything. In spite of everything—yes, that's the way one must put it.

When all the women arrived above the ravine, they came to a halt and stayed standing there. Without moving. Mute. What was to be done? What were they to do? For the dead of the ordinary sort one knows what to do. But for these . . . this enormous pile of dead. This huge heap.

We stayed there, our fingers loosening, our useless hands going slack. We forgot about the children, whom we ought to have spared this. It did not occur to us to send them home. Indeed, could we have? They were clinging to us. What were we to do now?

We didn't hesitate long, as I think back on it. First one, then another, then all of us made our way down into the ravine and went over to where the men lay

on top of each other

and when one recognized her husband

she'd pull him a little to one side

and each looked for her own

her husband, her father, or her son,

or all of them at once. I had five to find. Fortunately, they had stayed together, and I found them this way. My husband was still holding the hand of our youngest son. And my father-in-law . . . the man who knew how to talk to bees. He was always the one people came to see when the bees were supposed to swarm.

Three generations: husband, father, son. The same thing for the whole countryside.

Our town's memory was lost with the men who fell that day. There's no one left to remember just how the blacksmith used to hold the horseshoe. He was reputed for his skill. When he shoed a mule they made a circle round his forge to watch how he did it.

There is no one left to remember how the cabinet-maker aged his oak, and it's also an entire language that has been lost, the language of men's crafts. No one says any longer: "D'you remember Vassili, the blacksmith? How quickly he was able to straighten out a ploughshare? And Costa, the carpenter, how quickly he'd work a tree trunk into a beam with his adze! And how true the beam would be!" Those they had shared their skills with, the helpers who were to have taken over when they were gone—they all died together at the same time.

Bending over the tangled bodies, in the waning light of day's end, the women continued searching. It was wintertime. And if night were to fall before each had found her own . . .

And so our movements quickened. And then, as each one extricated hers from the pile of the dead, pulled him to one side, lay him on his back, it gradually became easier to sort through the diminishing pile.

At the same time, a glimmering of hope—hope is an incredible thing. You never quite believe in death, not right away; you hear the steps of the dead man in the house for a long time after you've buried him. You need time to get used to things,

and meanwhile an insane hope—that's how it is . . . these men were alive a little while ago, and now

here

fallen every which way, like drunks, one on top of the other, and still warm . . . Perhaps not every one of them was dead, perhaps underneath the dead a man would be found alive . . . We were almost envious of the woman for whom this mad hope might turn out to be true. Alas.

And the women stepped cautiously between the corpses, taking care not to get in each other's way, for there were hundreds of them, hundreds of women bending over those corpses

dark gleaners,

gatherers of the dead,

in this stony gully where for the first time a harvest was taking place.

They had tucked up their skirts so as not to soil them, but the earth had already imbibed all the blood and on the stones the blood had dried already.

The women moved cautiously from one man to another, gently turning face up those who had fallen face to the ground, and, upon recognizing this one or that one, announcing in a murmured

Antigone, your Costa,

Daphne, your Dimitri

and they continued their quest until each one had found hers or, most often, all of hers.

Without straightening up, the women proceeded step by step, at each step looking where to set their feet between the corpses.

We couldn't identify them from a distance, by their clothing. Here all the men dressed alike: black trousers, black jacket, white shirt. The same with the women: black dress, a black scarf upon the head.

And when she had found her man

each woman would gently lift him, gently lay him down on the ground, gently turn his head till it was straight, close his eyelids, and place her handkerchief over his face.

Wives would remove the wedding ring from their husband's finger before it stiffened, and slip their husband's ring on their own finger, next to theirs. Today, in our town, you come upon many women with two wedding bands on their ring-finger, women who're not yet so very old. They are that day's widows.

The betrothed took nothing. They simply helped the mothers lay out their sons, the young men they were betrothed to.

Then the women from the surrounding villages came running, worried that their men had not returned from market. When they found themselves in the deserted streets, with the houses empty, doors wide open

they knew at once a misfortune had befallen, and the old people keeping watch over the little ones told them to go to the hill.

Then

they also began to search through the pile of the dead, tenderly, humbly sorting through them, with attentive hands.

And the children were still there, doing their share of this work which was not meant for them. They learned more on that day than is needed for a whole lifetime.

And in this way night came on and we still didn't know what else to do.

So we walked back down,

except for two or three who had no one left at home and who wanted to weep by themselves. The ones who had little children at home

the children had to be fed

they started back down, stumbling in the dark, dead tired but suddenly devoid of any feeling, their hearts suddenly turned to stone.

And when the children had been put to bed, one of the women went from door to door. She had lighted a wax candle at the ever-burning flame under the icons.

Then each woman took a taper and put on a shawl

and we all went up to the ravine for the vigil. The old people joined us there, also with lighted candles.

The aged had a hard time climbing the rocky path, and those of us who were already at the top

watched the little trembling flames of the candles in the wavering procession mounting towards us.

The moon came up. The night grew bright. It was December.

The night was spent in prayers, barely whispered prayers. Each mourner knelt next to her own. Sometimes holding the hand of her husband or of her son

as though to keep the body from growing cold,

as though to maintain a bit of warmth in it for as long as possible, a semblance of life.

But in the morning a decision had to be arrived at.

We had to make up our minds what we were to do.

We hadn't spoken all night long. Each one, while praying, was thinking her own thoughts and nothing had been decided by the time the stars faded from the sky,

by the time the candles dripped their last drops of wax upon the stones where we had set them.

We walked back down to the town in silence.

Then someone said: "First we must ready them for burial. After that we will have to bury them."

Laying out a body for burial, everyone knows about that.

As for the burying itself . . .

The gravedigger was there, dead with the others.

And what gravedigger has ever buried thirteen hundred dead all at once? Who could dig thirteen hundred graves in a single day, particularly in our stony soil?

And the coffins? The carpenter was there, dead with the others.

What carpenter could build thirteen hundred coffins in a day? He'd never have the materials for thirteen hundred coffins. What carpenter ever stocks enough wood for thirteen hundred coffins all at once?

The carpenter, the smith, the farrier, the miller, the wheelwright, the woodcutter, they were all there, dead with the others.

And where would you bury them? There wasn't room enough in the cemetery for thirteen hundred graves. A cemetery is something that grows little by little over the years.

We couldn't just leave them there.

We didn't know how to bury them.

And it was as though they were dying a second time, by being there

dead,

deprived of the respects that are due to the dead.

Each dead man has the right to a coffin. But the carpenter was there, dead, and so was the blacksmith for the nails and the handles.

Each dead man has the right to a grave dug for him. But the gravedigger was there, and so were all those who would have helped dig.

Each dead man has the right to a funeral mass. But the priest was there too, among the dead.

Doesn't each dead man have the right to a final resting-place, a resting-place with a tombstone bearing his name? But the stonecutter was there as well, among the dead.

All the artisans were dead. To whom would the boys be apprenticed when they came of age?

Then one of the women said: "We must bury all of them together."

"Bury them where? You can't dig a hole in the stones at the bottom of the ravine."

"We must bury them all together, they died all together."

"Without coffins, without anything?"

"Without coffins, with our hands."

And—but exactly whose idea was it? I don't remember anymore. Perhaps it occurred to all of us together.

It was decided that we'd put them all together, as close together as we could possibly get them, and even, if that had to be, on top of one another, so that they'd fit into the square plot still vacant in the center of the cemetery. And that we wouldn't dig graves but that we'd construct a wall around them to make a kind of mausoleum. You saw it, didn't you? In the center of the cemetery, surrounded by cypress trees. It's not a handsome mausoleum. It's the best we were able to do at that time when materials were not easy to come by.

That's what was decided.

That's what we did.

We went home. The animals were in an uproar. They were hungry. The dogs were going crazy at the end of their chains. We fed all the animals. We fed the children. After that we went back to the ravine,

each with a pitcher of water,

a washcloth,

a sheet for the shroud.

We washed their faces,

we removed their shirts, sticky with blood, in order to wash their wounds,

because we couldn't let them go like this, with their wounds full of earth. Our warm tears fell upon their wounds,

and that is how we bade them farewell before wrapping them in the sheets.

When all was done, we took the litter on which coffins are borne in our town. Yes, that's still the practice here, we carry our dead upon our shoulders. And so, one by one, taking turns doing the carrying, we began transporting our dead to the square plot in the middle of the cemetery.

But to lift and carry thirteen hundred dead by taking them one at a time, could it be done? We realized we wouldn't be able to, that it would take days and days, even using two additional litters, hastily put together by the old men working in the carpenter's shop.

We saw we were never going to accomplish our task when reinforcements came from the neighboring villages, and we were able to finish before nightfall.

Someone went to fetch a monk from a monastery in the mountains. He had to go far because the two nearest monasteries had been set on fire and the monks hanged or thrown over cliffs. The barbarians had made a stop at the two monasteries before visiting us. The monasteries were on their way.

To find a monk meant going quite some distance. He did not arrive until late in the evening, as we were bearing the last litters.

The monk said prayers for all the dead together.

Then we went home. Those who no longer had anyone there didn't want to leave the cemetery. They lit a fire because of wild animals. The children went from house to house gathering wood and brought it for the fire.

And so it went until morning.

In the morning we knew what we had to do.

It was to build a dry wall, not very high, around the square plot, using the kind of stones we use for the retaining walls around our fields.

When the wall stood a little higher than the pile of dead, we covered the bodies with earth. We got the earth from our fields and carried it in baskets.

Until nightfall you saw a long procession of women each of whom carried all the earth she could,

earth scraped from the fields the men had plowed and sown the autumn before.

It was only later that we were able to have the wall raised the whole way and the mausoleum covered by a roof, as you see it today.

But we did our duty to our dead, rendering unto them all that which is owing to the dead.

We buried our dead as one must.

The monument on the hill, with all the names engraved on the walls, the monument you are looking at now was erected much later. The war had long since been over, the foreign soldiers with their boots and helmets had long since returned home, when the monument was put up.

In order that people remember.

Perhaps they, the soldiers, have forgotten. You forget when you have been ashamed.

For I can't believe they felt no shame, those young soldiers who killed men

and so many at one time, with all the blood that flowed,

that makes a lot of blood, thirteen hundred men,

killed men who might have been their fathers, and boys of their own age who might have been their brothers. No, I can't believe they felt no shame, those soldiers.

Farewell, traveler.

When you walk through the village to get back to the road and head homeward,

look at the clock on the public square. The time the clock shows is the time it happened that day. Something in the clock's mechanism broke with the first salvo. We haven't had it repaired.

It's the time it was that day.

XX

Kalavrita is a village in the Peloponnesus. It was in December of 1943.

XXI

"How can one continue to be German? After this, how can you remain German? I won't be able to be German any longer. I can't. I don't want to be." "What are you going to do not to be German?" "I'll go away." "A whole country can't emigrate. And I imagine it will take greater courage to stay than to leave." "Courage for what? In order to bear shame? In order to bear scorn? Courage to go on living with one's conscience? Thank you very much. I don't wish to display that kind of courage. It's hypocritical courage, fraudulent courage. Actually it's cowardice. You were in Auschwitz and you told me about it. It wasn't only Auschwitz. They're beginning to find out things in Berlin. Atrocious, unbelievable things. The whole face of Germany is covered with stinking abcesses, mass graves, branded everywhere with the shame of the camps. Right here in Ravensbrück, sixty kilometers outside Berlin, on the edge of the nice little town of Ravensbrück—for Berlin it's like Fontainebleau for Paris—right next to this forest for Sunday picnics, these atrocities: medical experiments, the elderly and the infirm sent off to unknown destinations: the secret shipments. You think it's not known? Everything is going to be known. Everything. And after that they'll find out what went on in the occupied countries: the SS divisions, killing, burning wherever they went. We still have a lot to find out. They say that in Tulle, in France . . . You know the city I'm talking about? All the men were hanged from the trees and streetlamps along the main street. We found out from wounded soldiers sent back from the Western front. Oh. I'm sorry . . . Perhaps you have family in Tulle."

"No, I don't know anyone there."

"It'll all come out. And the truth will have to be accepted. That's what's in store for the German people. If they don't feel guilty it's because they're lying. Can you go on lying to yourself indefinitely, saying *I didn't know*? The children's inheritance will be heavier than they can bear. How will they ever get rid of its weight? I don't want to have German children."

"Hannelore, you are here in Ravensbrück. You have been—you still are—a victim of the Nazis. Why should you have a guilty conscience?"

"The whole German people is going to have a guilty conscience. And every one of them is going to have to find some justification. I can't keep on wearing the Ravensbrück striped uniform to set myself apart from the guilty ones. Everyone is guilty, either of having taken part in the atrocities, or of having looked the other way while they were happening."

"I went through the ruins of Berlin when our little group was transferred from Auschwitz to Ravensbrück. I saw the long trains loaded with the wounded returning from the Eastern front. And those millions who were killed on the various fronts—a younger generation wiped out, countless families destroyed: isn't that enough to have paid?"

"The German dead will turn out to be nothing compared to the millions of Jews, Gypsies, women, children, old people the German army rounded up in every country it occupied. We'll never be able to pay for Auschwitz, Birkenau, Mauthausen, Bergen-Belsen and all the other places whose names have not yet been discovered but which will be, each with its thousands of tortured human beings, its mountains of corpses. The name of each camp will scar every German's flesh. We don't yet know how many of those camps there were. And when we find out . . . They're all over Germany, everywhere, and as Germany is a very densely populated country, people won't be able to claim those camps were in uninhabited areas. We don't have uninhabited areas here. And for obvious reasons, a camp is always on a railroad line. Sitting in the train, you look out and there the prisoners are, behind the electrified barbed wire fences. Out of habit I've been saying *we*. I don't want to have anything more to do with this *we*."

"Don't you want to differentiate, as I hope I'll be able to, between the Nazis and the German people?"

"And where do they come from, these Nazis, if not from the German people? And these swaggering young SS, arsonists, torturers, camp guards—they're not German? No, no. They're all in it together. They were all cowards. My father, for example. Yes, my father. He isn't a Nazi; he's a German. He isn't a Nazi but he took the oath of loyalty to Hitler. Necessarily, since he's a general in the German army. To be the daughter of a German army general and to be here, a prisoner—pretty funny, isn't it? You don't believe me? My father is German. So is my mother, but she's also Jewish. Here is how that is expressed today: my father is German, my mother is a German Jew. That means Jewish primarily and German after that. And yet, as far back as we can trace it, her people were German, like my father's. Her culture is German, her language is German. Germany is our country. My father, the son of an officer who fought in France in the First World War, is a professional soldier. My mother's a singer. Was a singer, I should say, for once the racial laws were promulgated—and who voted those laws through?—her singing engagements ended. Previously she had been famous, applauded, sought after. She had a name. During my childhood the red-letter days for me were my mother's departures and returns. I remember her getting her suitcase ready, the lovely dresses she had for performing in operas in provincial cities—in our country those opera houses are important places, and there I go again saying *our country*—and she was also invited abroad. I was so proud of her I didn't mind being left with my governess. I was just a little bit sad the first night. My governess would buy the newspapers where there were photos of my mother in a long evening gown, her arms full of magnificent flowers, smiling as she bowed from the stage. And her homecomings were such joyous occasions! She always brought back presents for me, and let me admire the ones she had received. She was beautiful, wonderfully elegant, and smelled so sweet! My father was proud of her also. Then all of a sudden, pouff. Nothing. The singing class she held at the conservatory was cancelled, her private students stopped taking lessons with her. 'She's Jewish.' Up until then no one had given it a thought, suddenly she was a leper. Her recordings were withdrawn from sale. The singer was no more, hadn't existed. Then the war broke out. We hadn't thought that German Jews were in any danger. The deporations began with foreign-born Jews, mostly Polish Jews. We were told they were being sent back to where they came from. My father, who at the time was a colonel, was in line for promotion to general. The authorities put it up to him: divorce or resign from the army. He divorced. I'll never forgive him for that."

"What could he have done?"

"You see, that's cowardliness. Everyone says to himself: *there isn't anything I can do*, and everybody knuckles under. What can one do? I don't know, but one should resist, say no. Out of pride. My father preferred to fight for Hitler, to take part in a vile war, and at the highest military level. Had he refused all three of us might have been interned. Well?"

"Your mother would have been sent to Auschwitz. Soon after our group got there we saw a big convoy of Berlin Jewish women arrive."

"Come on, it's not because my father divorced her that mother wasn't deported! It's because she went into hiding. Both of us were in hiding, separately, my mother in one place, I in another. I know she's still in a little town in the south, living with very close friends. I remained in Berlin, under the roof of some people we actually hardly knew at all: former socialists, both of them retired professors, who did what they could to fight against the prevailing madness. At that time, it was mostly a matter of fighting against official propaganda, of pointing out the truth the communiqués masked. A difficult business, especially since the bombings kept us forever on the move. Three times, the houses where we lived were bombed flat. That caused us to lose contact with the members of our network, if you can call that group a network. Constant moving and air raids did have one advantage: the police could no longer keep track. You can't imagine what

Berlin was like during those last months of the war: chaos amidst the wreckage. The height of mockery for your law-and-order loving German. And somehow life still went on. Burglaries, looting, common criminals escaping from jails blown wide open, gangs of thieves practically operating in broad daylight. Let me tell you, those were exciting times despite the fear, despite the ever more frequent alerts, despite the misery. And for those of us who, like my friends and I were waiting for the end of Hitler, for the end of the war, for the defeat of the German army, each Anglo-American air raid was a joy. An insane city.

"Via indirect means I received money from my father from time to time. I impatiently awaited the end of the war. Hitler is obviously beaten, I told myself, he'll never recover. The Russian army is in Poland, Paris has been liberated. Soon you'll be home. So I waited for the end of the war, pleased to have remained in Berlin until the very last. I wanted to see the Allies march into Berlin, Hitler chained to the conquerors' chariot, the windbag deflated, me in the front row of the crowd to jeer at him and spit in his face—and then there was the attempt on Hitler's life last July, and, after it, the huge roundups the Gestapo and the military police staged throughout the city. The people I was staying with were arrested despite the fact they had not had the faintest involvement in the plot. It was something the military cooked up all by themselves. I was arrested also. I don't know where they are. They weren't Jewish. So far as the law is concerned, I am a half-Jew. As such I was entitled to Ravensbrück and not to a death camp. One can hope to get out of here alive. If I can find Mother, we'll both leave. If I do not find her, I'll leave alone."

"Where will you go?"

"To the United States. I have done a little acting. I'd love to do something in the movies."

I ran into Hannelore two years later, in Paris. She was on her way to New York. With her flaming red hair, almond-shaped grey eyes, milk-white skin and heavily made-up mouth, her plan to go to Hollywood didn't seem a bit outrageous, as it had in

Ravensbrück, where, however, she had been among the least ravaged of the prisoners, having been arrested only shortly before.

"Did you find your mother again?"

"Yes."

"Is she leaving with you?"

"Can you believe that my father was denazified! Yes, he insisted on it, although he had never joined the Nazis; but once burned, twice shy. For a general, a piece of official paper with a red seal, that's what counts. And of course he had his divorce annulled with no trouble. My mother's back with him. She still loves him. Imagine that! In a way, she is his conscience. She can't sing any longer. She lost her voice. And yet her career ought not to be finished. She's still young."

"And you, are you making a clean break with Germany, as you had decided?"

"Germany . . . if you could see the place. Black marketeering everywhere, intrigues to get whitewashed. No one was ever a Nazi. Not a soul. They're on their knees before the Americans, their wealth, their cigarettes, their cans of food. It's disgusting. There are those who are patching things slowly, silently, and others who'll never get over it. There are the usual go-getters who always manage. One tries to live in the midst of all that. With this weight on one's heart, the eternal mourning. With those who died on the battlefield, in camps, in the bombing raids, as prisoners, there are few families that have remained intact. At this point we're gluing the pieces back together. Once this has been accomplished, remorse will strangle the Germans. You cannot erase history. The day will come when they will have to answer their children's questions."

Torture in Algeria.
My language has been appropriated by the executioners.
Villages burned by napalm in Indochina.
Algerians hunted through the streets by the Paris police one
day in October of 1961.
Algerians whose bodies were fished out of the Seine.
How often I have thought of you, Hannelore.

When we emerged from the camps, run down to the point of stupor, we had not even the strength to feel joy. Just to rest, to sleep, sleep our fill. Never, it seemed to us, would our tiredness go away. Nor our sadness. Upon us lay the weight of all those who were not returning. A few thousand survivors as against millions of dead, a sum of suffering that will never be reckoned, by anyone. We, though, we were going home and life would resume. We still didn't have a very clear understanding of it. All the things we had planned to do, all our dreams of how it would be afterward faded into a mist of unreality. Our preoccupations did not extend beyond the immediate: slaking our thirst, sleeping, eating, not hearing the siren anymore, not commanding our bodies to keep upright, to keep walking; ceasing that exhausting supervision of our every gesture, ceasing to be eternally on the alert; letting go, relaxing. That is, not having to worry about everything. For my part, I felt that, no longer stiffened by my efforts of will, my limbs were going slack, my backbone was melting.

In the confused state we were all in, certain things did however stand out clearly: the guards' watch towers were collapsing, barbed wire enclosures were toppling, the camps were being swept away by a cleansing whirlwind: victory. Grass would sprout on the mustering grounds. The enormous sores that had disfigured vast stretches of territory would be effaced by vegetation, covered by earth's natural mantle. Victory had been costly, but it was here at last, glowing. Freedom had been won. Our dead, our millions of dead, our suffering, our humiliation would be inscribed in history. We were coming back. We had a tale to tell.

We'd tell it later on. For the moment the thing to do was get our strength back, get our bearings, get back into the mainstream of life, into our former life or a new one: marry, have children, work, embark on studies or take them up again, return to an old job or switch to another to make a fresh start. Slowly our thinking began to revive. You had to reconstruct your personality, so to speak. That is, you had to resume possession of yourself, collecting the scattered pieces which reappeared all of a sudden or else came back to light little by little, pieces you had believed lost and that you had now to stick back together, as you did so erasing the scars left by the camp. And so once home again, each of us was seen to go his own way; those who had been inseparable companions now sometimes went for years without seeing one another. Each was too much taken up with all the problems he was beset by, unforeseen difficulties very often of the most prosaic sort. No, it wasn't self-centeredness, self-absorption. Europe was picking up the wreckage, criminals were being brought to justice and sentenced; history had no further need of us. The next generation would grow up in freedom.

Everyone wanted life to pleasant and nice again, wanted the comforts of old habits, illusions, beliefs, dreams.

When the raw reality was revealed about the country which, since 1917, had represented the hope of the world's disinherited, when the truth about things in the Soviet Union finally burst into the open, many refused to believe it: it meant relinquishing their faith, the very purpose of their lives, the reason for which some had taken such great risks and had been deported.

A lofty, clear voice rose up then, so high and clear that it drowned out those which earlier had whispered the same truth: there are concentration camps in the USSR. Such was the ring of sincerity in this voice, such was its truthfulness that it was impossible to impugn its testimony, impossible to ignore it. From one end to the other of a land as vast as a continent stretched an archipelago of leprous islands, evil places with watch towers and barbed wire, camps enclosing men, women, adolescents, even children, millions of people.

Following his, other voices arose—just as clear, just as true. In the camps where the regime was the harshest deportees in striped prison garb like ours were being worked to death. They were being marched in columns five abreast, to the commands of dehumanized brutes, just as we had been marched in the Nazi camps. From east to west they extended, and into the far north—and in that country north means the Arctic Circle. For half a century, the living dead had been mining gold in the Kolyma region, the very gold out of which Lenin declared that urinals should be fashioned. Supreme derision. The balance sheet was frightful. Millions of dead, whole ethnic groups wiped out of existence, republics expunged from official maps.

We victims of a bloodthirsty madman, we who thought that this bloodthirsty madman's downfall meant the end of the concentration-camp system—here then is the truth we must live with now: camps still exist. An unbearable truth.

To tear down our barbed wire called for the combined effort of the most powerful nations, it required their armies, the mobilization of all their industrial might, and the resistance of subjugated peoples. But for the military victory we would all have perished.

We, caged behind our barbed wire, we were able to count on Hitler's eventual defeat. For us it was a certainty. Hope gave us the strength to hang on. We did not know for how long we would have to endure—victory sometimes seemed so far off that we feared we would no longer be alive to see it—as alas turned out to be true for most of us—; but our certainty remained. Hitler will be crushed, we'll pull through.

What then of the prisoners in Siberian camps, condemned for years and years? How do they hang on? What hope gives them the strength to fight to survive until a liberation which keeps receding all the time? Who'll get them out of there? Who will tear down the watch towers and the wire? When, thanks to what circumstances, will the concentration-camp system—this shame we associated only with Nazism—be abolished? No one will wage a war for their sake, there is no sign of the political system collapsing, our protests are ineffectual.

The frozen songs of the Kolyma freeze our hearts.

Comrades, O my comrades, we who swore not to forget our dead, what can we do for these forgotten souls? Some of them are yet alive. Some of them continue to hope.